Advance Reviews

I've had the opportunity to interview Richard on my radio show (Rush To Reason) weekly for the past year. We have talked through many topics to help my listeners and business leaders work through the many challenges we have all faced this past year. His weekly words of wisdom and encouragement have helped me and my listeners navigate through life.

Richard was also very comforting to me personally these past few months when my brother, who was dying from brain cancer, went to be with the Lord. His positive outlook on life is and was a huge encouragement to my entire family and me.

Richard is a man of integrity who understands success and failure, joy and sorrow, having much and also had little. He is a man you can count on to calm the storm always. I'm sure all of us will find daily words of wisdom and encouragement in his new book *Life's Daily Treasure* – I know I will.

- John W. Rush, Radio Host/ Business Owner, and Coach

"Richard's latest book is an enchanting compendium of insight, wisdom, and inspiration. The elegant simplicity of his approach for *Life's Daily Treasure* belies the genius of his strategy. I was so intrigued with how well he researched and coordinated all this content around motivational themes! Whether you read it straight through or savor it day by day, you're sure to be delighted with his medley of motivation and optimism. What an incredible gift to share with your loved ones."

- Christina J. Moore, Apr. – Lecturer, McCoy College of Business, Texas State University

As I began reading the monthly inspirations, I felt my spirits lifted. As an author myself, I especially enjoyed this particular Battle's Bullet - 'If you don't receive the fruit of your labor immediately, do not become discouraged but stay the course.' There are many times when I do feel this way. Battle's words encouraged me to 'stay the course.'

If you are in need of inspiration, pick up this book. You will feel the inspiration flowing throughout your being. I highly recommend this book by this inspirational and motivational author. He has several other books that will inspire you also. This is a beautiful book that will continue to provide encouragement to you whenever you need it.

We all need to be inspired so that we can continue living full and rich lives. Thank you, Richard Battle, for being that inspiration!

- Janice Spina, multi-award-winning author of 35 books

Richard Battle has created a uniquely useful book for those of us who like a touch of inspiration with our morning coffee. "Life's Daily Treasure" is one part devotional, one part sage advice, and a third-part factoid. And it's all served up in an easy-to-digest format that's quick to read but offering ample opportunity for contemplation and journaling.

- Charles Besondy, award-winning author of Christian fiction

Richard has created a unique book with devotionals, historical resources, motivational quotes, and a personal journal for each day of the year. The book is inspiring, motivating, and fun. It will be a valuable resource for executives, students, and retirees!

- Rick Rhodes, **4-term mayor, Sweetwater, Texas**

This may be the best of the eight books that Richard has blessed all of us with his publishing..... because of its simplicity and "readability." It combines all of the principles of leadership that

Richard has written about and that he lives, with the thought that we will have greater peace in our personal lives and greater success in our business lives if we live each day with God as our Center. I anxiously await getting my early copy of "Life's Daily Treasure"..... and begin each day with the spiritual message of that day.

- Wayne T Franke, MJWT Consulting

ALSO, BY RICHARD V. BATTLE

Navigating Life's Journey – Common Sense in Uncommon Times

Conquering Life's Course – Common Sense in Chaotic Times

Unwelcome Opportunity – Overcoming Life's Greatest Challenges

Surviving Grief by God's Grace

The Master's Sales Secrets

The Four-Letter Word That Builds Character

The Volunteer Handbook – How to Organize and Manage A Successful Organization

LIFE'S DAILY
Treasure

366 Doses of
Hope, **O**ptimism,
Personal Growth and
Encouragement

LIFE'S DAILY
Treasure

366 Doses of
Hope, **O**ptimism,
Personal Growth and
Encouragement

Richard V. Battle

Life's Daily Treasure
366 Doses of Hope, Optimism, Personal Growth and Encouragement
All Rights Reserved.
Copyright © 2021 Richard V. Battle
v3.0 r1.0

The opinions expressed in this manuscript are solely the opinions of the author and do not represent the opinions or thoughts of the publisher. The author has represented and warranted full ownership and/or legal right to publish all the materials in this book.

This book may not be reproduced, transmitted, or stored in whole or in part by any means, including graphic, electronic, or mechanical without the express written consent of the publisher except in the case of brief quotations embodied in critical articles and reviews.

Outskirts Press, Inc.
http://www.outskirtspress.com

Paperback ISBN: 978-1-9772-4471-0
Hardback ISBN: 978-1-9772-3881-8

Copyright Registration: TXu 2-259-792

Library of Congress Control Number: 2021911419

Cover Photo © 2021 Shutterstock.com. All rights reserved - used with permission.

All Scripture quotations, unless otherwise noted, are taken from *The Holy Bible, New International Version* from www.biblegateway.com

Outskirts Press and the "OP" logo are trademarks belonging to Outskirts Press, Inc.

PRINTED IN THE UNITED STATES OF AMERICA

Dedication

Thank you to all whose shoulders I stand on, known and unknown who made my path easier. May I return the favor by broadening my shoulders to ease the way for others who follow me.

To you who discover this volume. It is dedicated to providing daily-treasures for readers to expand their horizons and enrich their lives.

May you find seeds within it that benefit you and all those you touch for years to come.

Table of Contents

Preface	i
Introduction	iii
Acknowledgments	vii
Cover Photo Story	ix
Rear Cover and Interior Photo	xi
Daily Legend	xvii
Month	
January	1
February	33
March	63

April	95
May	127
June	159
July	191
August	223
September	255
October	287
November	319
December	351
Bibliography	383
About the Author	387
Richard V. Battle Resources	389

Preface

You will note a common theme with two previous volumes for those familiar with my earlier authorship.

Life's Daily Treasure is a humble companion to ***Conquering Life's Course: Common Sense in Chaotic Times*** and ***Navigating Life's Journey: Common Sense in Uncommon Times.*** I plan to add a final volume to this series.

The other volumes include significant parts of my life experience supplemented with historical and contemporary individuals. It reflects my love for my country, its history, and its contributions to humanity's advancement.

I discovered late my life mission to **Provide Timeless Positive Messages of Proven Principles Helping People Win Every day! My contribution in this volume is Battle's Bullets, taken from my previous writings, presentations, and communications.**

From, *The Volunteer Handbook: How to Organize and Manage a Successful Organization*, through *Surviving Grief by God's Grace, The Four-Letter Word that Builds Character, The Master's Sales Secrets, Unwelcome Opportunity: Overcoming Life's Greatest Challenges, Conquering Life's Course: Common Sense in Chaotic Times* and *Navigating Life's Journey: Common Sense in Uncommon Times*, I strive to offer principles and ideas contributing to people's personal growth.

I'm blessed to communicate my messages via written books in the paper, audio and electronic versions, public speaking, radio and television appearances, and online video. The mode of communication is not as important to me as reaching as many people as possible with positive ideas for their benefit.

I thrive on discovering new ideas and embarking on new projects. To me, life is an adventure to its very end. Anything less is a wasted opportunity for us and those we may positively impact along the way.

Life should be a one-way trip of growth and exploration, lived with enthusiasm, resilience, and persistence to our last breath. Ralph Waldo Emerson was prescient when he stated, "The mind once stretched by a new idea, never returns to its original dimensions.

My hope is your journey is exciting and happy, and your experience with my messages adds value to it.

Remember, it's not where we've been nor where we are that counts, but where we finish. Let's all complete our missions victoriously!

Introduction

Life can become a daily grind, discouraging the pursuit of one's dreams and the belief in humanity's goodness.

Life's obstacles come large and small, short and long term, and can attack us mentally, physically, spiritually, emotionally, or all of the above.

We all need a periodic lift of our spirits, not only to get through our daily routines but to relentlessly pursue our dreams to improve our lives and the lives of others.

This volume is a small effort to provide positivity in a world where adverse reporting reigns, and encourages people to dream big in a world of discouragement. It aims to inspire people to dream and act big because you never know what you can achieve until you give it everything you have until your final breath.

It combines my love for America and its history, motivation, personal growth, and inspiration. Its basis is a reverence for the contributions of people who built the most prosperous and successful country in the world's history utilizing principles and values constructed over thousands of years by millions of people. They understood human nature, acknowledged their imperfections, and lived their best lives, knowing they could not change it.

You will discover this volume is part **Almanac, Commemoration, Celebration, Motivation, Personal journal** for recording personal anniversaries and observations**, and all Inspirational.**

It is not designed for any single year but enables you to refer to its page's year-after-year for renewed **Hope**, **Optimism**, **Personal Growth**, and **Encouragement**, which are its theme.

Each day's offering includes six parts and follows one of 31 daily subjects. The six components are **Inspiration, National Day** celebration, Historical **Anniversary, Born Today, Motivation, and Battle's Bullet**. There is also a place to record **personal observations** for each date.

You'll note there isn't room for detailing any of the listings. The wisdom of the ages is accessible at our fingertips. Readers can search the internet for additional information to feed their interest.

Inspiration is based on Biblical Scriptures from 49 books and will inspire and lift the readers' spirit based on the 31 daily subjects I emphasize.

While some organizations recognize multiple **National Day** observations, I have selected one to commemorate each day in this volume.

Anniversaries of events were generally selected to appreciate the positive contributions those people and their actions have made to our country.

Born Today champions individuals to appreciate their contributions to others and society.

Included **Motivational Quotes** also reflect each day's topic and compliments the inspirational Scripture.

Battle's Bullets are comments I made in previous books and messages emphasizing each day's subject.

The Personal Observance is a space where you can log memorable events in your life as an annual reminder. Readers might also find it beneficial to record what the listings mean to them or other individual thoughts from a day.

My desire is the information in this volume will lift your spirit, inspire you to pursue your dreams, and increase your pride in your country and fellow man. You will see ordinary people who achieved extraordinary achievements and in them find inspiration for each day.

Acknowledgments

I'm so grateful once again to my family for their continued support, assistance, and commitment. They have stood by me through success and failure, trial and triumph. Thank you especially to my daughter Elizabeth, and brother Jerry and sister-in-law Cheryl Battle. I'm appreciative of my father, Bill, who I quoted, and my other ancestors who gave of themselves so unselfishly for my benefit.

Words continue to be insufficient to communicate my gratitude for this volume and associated projects for the invaluable guidance and feedback of my long-time friend, mentor, and pastor Dr. Logan Cummings.

I appreciate the encouraging comments during this project from Leslie Siller, Jim McGee and Larry Coulter.

Thank you to Burke Allen Adkins and Shaili Priya at Allen Media Strategies for their contributions to this volume and my speaking endeavors.

I appreciate Alane Pearce's consultation and editing of the manuscript. Her suggestions were invaluable.

Thank you to the team at Outskirts Press, including Jamie Belt and Lisa Jones, for their assistance in bringing this project to life.

Most importantly, I'm grateful for the inspiration and provision from my Heavenly Father for this volume. Any shortcomings in it are all mine as in all things. As the epitaph on the marker of my future resting place says, "For that, I did well credit God, the rest me."

Cover Photo Story

Licensed by Shutterstock **226913857**

If you have read any book, I authored beginning with my second, ***Surviving Grief by God's Grace***, you probably noticed thematic cover photos.

I didn't begin with a plan to utilize one theme. In reality, I didn't pre-plan as many books as I have published to date.

All but one portrays nature, utilizing the metaphor of our life's journey. Regardless of where we are on our pilgrimage, the messages are the same. The only difference is how we receive the information based on our previous life experiences and view of life.

The pictures chosen for this cover and back cover/interior were deliberate and designed to utilize the metaphor of discovering a life-changing treasure.

The open treasure chest sitting on the beach conveys the ease of its access. The gold contents reveal its value, which is beyond mere money. The treasure is worth much more in changing its finder's quality of life and the lives of all he or she impacts for years beyond their lifetime.

More important than gold or silver are inspirational ideas that transform us into more significant people than we were before we learned their secrets.

The bright sun, sky, clouds, and ocean unveil the limitless potential of our lives. Despite discouragement and setbacks, we are never more than one achievement away from resuming our pursuit of accomplishing our goals and dreams.

The treasure chest lies on the beach, inviting us to explore and implement its contents to elevate our pursuit of happiness. The choice is ours on how we use the treasure

Rear Cover and Interior Photo

Licensed by **Shutterstock 541520356**

Searching for treasure or pursuing one's dreams requires a map and compass to reach the desired destination as quickly as possible.

The image on the back cover and interior pages displays a map and compass as a reminder to define our objective, map a course to reach it, and utilize the appropriate tools to ensure success.

Whether we plan our journey early in life or adjust our course later, as long as breath remains in us, we may alter our direction onto a more profitable pathway.

--

My mission is to provide timeless messages of proven principles helping people win every day.

Life's Daily Treasure and my other efforts aim to share my love for personal growth and life-transforming ideas with as many people as possible.

I hope you will reap the rewards of the treasure within these pages and share them with as many people as you touch during your lives. If we both pass along the wisdom within these pages, we will make a difference during our time on Earth.

May God bless you and all of your endeavors!

Life's Daily Treasure

366 Doses

Of

Hope, **O**ptimism, **P**ersonal growth and **E**ncouragement

Description

Part Almanac, Historic Celebration, Personal Journal, Trivia, and all Inspirational.

Themes

Hope
Optimism
Personal Growth
Encouragement

366 Daily Components

Scripture	Inspiration – 49 books of *The Bible* are quoted
National Day	Celebration
Anniversary	Historical Commemoration
Born Today	Contributor to American Success

Quote   Motivation
Battle's Bullet   Action Item
Personal Observance Personal Events

31 Daily Subjects

Legend of Subjects and Monthly Date

Subject	Date
Joy	1
Honor	2
Heart	3
Hope	4
Courage	5
Act	6
Fearless	7
Humble	8
Faith- Faithful	9
Provision	10
Mercy	11
Forgiveness	12
Grace	13
Love	14
Rejoice	15
Adversity – Obstacle – Trials	16
Encouragement	17
Endurance	18
Example	19
Grow	20
Overcomer	21

Patience	22
Peace	23
Stand Firm	24
Wisdom	25
Perseverance	26
Trustworthy/Trust	27
Truth – 2X	28
Victorious	29
Thankful	30
Good Cheer	31

Daily Legend

Month  Date

Daily Subject

Inspiration:	Biblical Scripture highlighting the daily subject
National Day:	One of the recognized national daily celebrations
Anniversary:	Positive American historical event
Born Today:	Celebrating the birth of an American who contributed to the building of our country.
Motivation:	Motivational quote highlighting the daily subject
Battle's Bullet:	Author's daily subject contribution from previous works and my Dear John letter to my late son

Personal Observances:
Reader-added information such as personal reflections, family birthdays, anniversaries, weddings, celebrations, etc.

JANUARY

January 1

Joy

Inspiration: **Genesis 1:1** - In the beginning God created the heavens and the earth.

National Day: New Year's Day

Anniversary: 1808 – Congress prohibits the importation of slaves

Born Today: 1735 – Paul Revere
1752 – Betsy Ross

Motivation: "Joy is the holy fire that keeps our purpose warm and our intelligence aglow." – Helen Keller

Battle's Bullet: The more we FIND to laugh about the happier we will be.

Personal Observances:
_____
_____
_____

January  2

Honor

Inspiration: Exodus 20:12 - "Honor your father and your mother, so that you may live long in the land the Lord your God is giving you."

National Day: National Science Fiction Day

Anniversary: 1906 – Willis Carrier receives a patent for the first air conditioner

Born Today: 1857 – Martha Carey Thomas - educator

Motivation: "It's not hard to make decisions when you know what your values are." – Roy F. Disney

Battle's Bullet: Never speak ill of others.

Personal Observances:

_____
_____
_____

January  3

Heart

Inspiration: Matthew 6:21 - For where your treasure is, there your **heart** will be also.

National Day: National Drinking Straw Day

Anniversary: 1823 – Stephen F. Austin receives a land grant in Texas from Mexico

Born Today: 1879 – Grace Coolidge – First Lady

Motivation: "Often the people with the most beautiful hearts are the ones who have endured the greatest pain." – Karen Salmansohn

Battle's Bullet: We should always help who we can, where we can, how we can.

Personal Observances:
_____
_____
_____

January  4

Hope

Inspiration: **Hebrews 11:1** -Now faith is confidence in what we **hope** for and assurance about what we do not see.

National Day: National Trivia Day

Anniversary: 1847 – Samuel Colt sells his first revolver to the U.S. government

Born Today: 1746 – Benjamin Rush – Statesman and Signer of Declaration of Independence

Motivation: "When the world says, 'Give up,' Hope whispers, 'Try it one more time.'" – Unknown

Battle's Bullet: Where we place our Hope is as important as the attitude of Hope itself!

Personal Observances:
_____
_____
_____

January 5

Courage

Inspiration: Joshua 1:7 - "Be strong and very **courage**ous. Be careful to obey all the law my servant Moses gave you; do not turn from it to the right or to the left, that you may be successful wherever you go."

National Day: National Whipped Cream Day

Anniversary: 1914 – Henry Ford provides workers $ 5 per day minimum wage, which was much higher than the current market.

Born Today: 1779 – Zebulon Pike – Army/explorer, Pike's Peak named for him

Motivation: "Courage is fear holding on a minute longer." – Xitclub.com

Battle's Bullet: Life is not fair. It doesn't matter which party is running the government. Get over it.

Personal Observances:
_____
_____
_____

January 6

Act

Inspiration: **Psalm 106:3** - Blessed are those who **act** justly, who always do what is right.

National Day: National Cuddle Up Day

Anniversary: 1838 – Samuel Morse first demonstrates his telegraph machine

Born Today: 1882 – Sam Rayburn – Speaker of the House of Representatives

Motivation: "You don't have to be great to start, but you have to start to be great." – Zig Ziglar

Battle's Bullet: Work is the four-letter word that builds character.

Personal Observances:
_____
_____
_____

January 7

Fearless

Inspiration: **Exodus 20:20** - Moses said to the people, "Do **not** be afraid. God has come to test you, so that the **fear** of God will be with you to keep you from sinning."

National Day: National Bobblehead Day

Anniversary: 1894 – Thomas Edison copyrights his first film, which was a five second clip

Born Today: 1800 – President Millard Fillmore (13)

Motivation: "The key to success is to focus our conscious mind on things we desire not things we fear." – Brian Tracy

Battle's Bullet: My faith enables me to live without fear of what may happen here and to look forward to what will happen for eternity.

Personal Observances:

_____
_____
_____

January  8

Humble

Inspiration:	**2 Chronicles 7:14** - if my people, who are called by my name, will **humble** themselves and pray and seek my face and turn from their wicked ways, then I will hear from heaven, and I will forgive their sin and will heal their land.
National Day:	National Bubble Bath Day
Anniversary:	1815 – Battle of New Orleans (despite war ending in December of 1814)
Born Today:	1935 – Elvis Presley - entertainer
Motivation:	"I humble myself before God and there the list ends." – Sam Houston
Battle's Bullet:	We are no better and no worse than anyone else.

Personal Observances:

_____
_____
_____

January 9

Faith - Faithful

Inspiration:	**Deuteronomy 7:9** - Know therefore that the Lord your God is God; he is the **faithful** God, keeping his covenant of love to a thousand generations of those who love him and keep his commandments.
National Day:	National Law Enforcement Day
Anniversary:	2007 – Founder of Apple, Steve Jobs, introduces the iPhone
Born Today:	1913 – President Richard Nixon (37)
Motivation:	"Don't miss out on a blessing because it isn't packaged the way you expected; expect the unexpected." – Lyndsey Baigent
Battle's Bullet:	God exists. Have faith, pray, and listen.

Personal Observances:

_____
_____
_____

January  10

Provision

Inspiration: **Genesis 50:21** - So then, don't be afraid. I will **provide** for you and your children." And he reassured them and spoke kindly to them.

National Day: National Cut Your Energy Costs Day

Anniversary: 1776 – *Common Sense* pamphlet is published by Thomas Paine

Born Today: 1738 – Ethan Allen – Revolutionary War patriot

Motivation: "God will carry you through a storm." – Isaiah 43:2

Battle's Bullet: Our civilization's norms are still worthy of implementing as our bedrock, providing us the sure footing and stability to modify the margins.

Personal Observances:
_____
_____
_____

January  11

Mercy

Inspiration: **Psalm 4:1** - Answer me when I call to you, my righteous God. Give me relief from my distress; have **mercy** on me and hear my prayer.

National Day: National Human Trafficking Awareness Day

Anniversary: 1935 – Amelia Earhart flies from Honolulu to Oakland

Born Today: 1755 – Alexander Hamilton, Founder/1st Treasury Secretary

Motivation: "Sweet mercy is nobility's true badge." – William Shakespeare

Battle's Bullet: The Lord had answered my prayers and granted me mercy. He always loves me more than I deserve!

Personal Observances:
_____
_____
_____

January  12

Forgiveness

Inspiration: **Psalm 79:9** - Help us, God our Savior, for the glory of your name; deliver us and **forgive** our sins for your name's sake.

National Day: National Sunday Supper Day

Anniversary: 1939 – Timely Comics, later Marvel, founded by Martin Goodman

Born Today: 1588 – John Winthrop – first governor of Massachusetts Bay Colony

Motivation: "Forgiveness is not about the person who wronged you. Forgiveness is about your heart being right with God." – Eva Conner

Battle's Bullet: The pain of regret is deeper and lasts longer than the pain of failure. We can forgive ourselves also.

Personal Observances:
_____
_____
_____

January 13

Grace

Inspiration:	**John 1:14** - The Word became flesh and made his dwelling among us. We have seen his glory, the glory of the one and only Son, who came from the Father, full of **grace** and truth.
National Day:	National Clean Off Your Desk Day
Anniversary:	1928 – GE and RCA install three test television sets in New York
Born Today:	1832 – Horatio Alger - author
Motivation:	"Grace is the only thing that is ever enough." – Ann Voskamp
Battle's Bullet:	Watch your expectations of others. They are only human and will let you down if you expect them to be perfect.

Personal Observances:

_____

_____

_____

January 14

Love

Inspiration:	**1 John 4:19** - We **love** because he first **love**d us.
National Day:	National Dress Up Your Pet Day
Anniversary:	1784 – U. S. Congress ratifies the Treaty of Paris ending The Revolutionary War
Born Today:	1892 – Hal Roach – movie producer and director
Motivation:	"Love is the sum of all virtue, and love disposes us to good." – Jonathan Edwards
Battle's Bullet:	Institutions come and go. The only thing that lasts is the relationships you make and what you learn from the experience.

Personal Observances:
_____
_____
_____

January  15

Rejoice

Inspiration:	**Psalm 32:11** - **Rejoice** in the Lord and be glad, you righteous; sing, all you who are upright in heart!
National Day:	National Hat Day
Anniversary:	1861 – Elisha Otis patents the first steam elevator
Born Today:	1929 – Martin Luther King Jr.
Motivation:	"I rejoice in what I have, and I greet the new with open arms." – Louise Hay
Battle's Bullet:	Happy is the heart that is thankful in all things.

Personal Observances:

_____
_____
_____

January 16

Adversity – Trials - Obstacles

Inspiration:	**Proverbs 17:17** - A friend loves at all times, and a brother is born for a time of **adversity**.
National Day:	National Religious Freedom Day
Anniversary:	1919 – 18th Amendment to Constitution prohibiting alcohol is ratified
Born Today:	1935 – A. J. Foyt - racing
Motivation:	"In the middle of every difficulty lies opportunity." – Albert Einstein
Battle's Bullet:	The real test of a person's character is how he/she responds to adversity.

Personal Observances:
_____
_____
_____

January  17

Encouragement

Inspiration: **Romans 15:5** - May the God who gives endurance and **encouragement** give you the same attitude of mind toward each other that Christ Jesus had

National Day: National Hot Buttered Rum Day

Anniversary: 1928 – First totally automatic film processing machine is patented

Born Today: 1706 – Benjamin Franklin

Motivation: "A word of encouragement during failure is worth more than an hour of praise after success." – geckoandfly.com

Battle's Bullet: Encouragement is the greatest gift we can give anyone.

Personal Observances:
_____
_____
_____

January  18

Endurance

Inspiration: **2 Samuel 7:16** - Your house and your kingdom will **endure** forever before me; your throne will be established forever.'"

National Day: National Use Your Gift Card Day

Anniversary: 1903 – First transatlantic radio transmission originating from the U.S was made

Born Today: 1782 – Daniel Webster – law, politics

Motivation: "Life is not about waiting for the storm to pass, but learning to dance in the rain." – Unknown

Battle's Bullet: Things can always be worse.

Personal Observances:
___
___
___

January  19

Example

Inspiration: John 13:15 - I have set you an **example** that you should do as I have done for you.

National Day: National Popcorn Day

Anniversary: 1955 – First televised presidential news conference

Born Today: 1809 – Edgar Allen Poe - author

Motivation: "Example, whether it be good or bad, has a powerful influence." – President George Washington

Battle's Bullet: Focus up and out, act, grow and repeat.

Personal Observances:

_____
_____
_____

January  20

Grow

Inspiration: **Psalm 92:12** - The righteous will flourish like a palm tree, they will **grow** like a cedar of Lebanon;

National Day: Martin Luther King Jr. Day

Anniversary: 1937 – First presidential inauguration after moving from March 4th

Born Today: 1930 – Buzz Aldrin – astronaut, the second person to set foot on the moon

Motivation: "Strength and growth come only from continued effort and struggle." – Napoleon Hill

Battle's Bullet: The only dog that can't learn a new trick is a dead dog.

Personal Observances:
_____
_____
_____

January 21

Overcomer

Inspiration: **Genesis 32:28** - Then the man said, "Your name will no longer be Jacob, but Israel, because you have struggled with God and with humans and have **overcome**."

National Day: National Hugging Day

Anniversary: 1954 – USS Nautilus - First U.S. nuclear power submarine is launched

Born Today: 1813 – John C. Fremont - explorer, military, politics

Motivation: "The struggle you're in today is developing the strength you need for tomorrow." – Unknown

Battle's Bullet: The earlier you face rejection and learn how to respond to it, the better you will be prepared for it when it comes again in the future.

Personal Observances:
_____
_____
_____

January 22

Patience

Inspiration: **Proverbs 19:11** - A person's wisdom yields **patience**; it is to one's glory to overlook an offense.

National Day: National Sanctity of Human Life Day

Anniversary: 1970 – First commercial 747 flight from New York to London

Born Today: 1904 – George Balanchine - music

Motivation: "Just because something isn't happening for you right now doesn't mean that it will never happen." – Unknown

Battle's Bullet: Like many other characteristics essential to our success and happiness, patience is one that we are not born with but hopefully will learn through the rigors of experience.

Personal Observances:
___
___
___

January 23

Peace

Inspiration:	**Psalm 29:11** - The Lord gives strength to his people; the Lord blesses his people with **peace**.
National Day:	National Pie Day
Anniversary:	1789 – Georgetown is founded as the first Catholic university in U.S.
Born Today:	1737 – John Hancock – patriot and first signer of Declaration of Independence
Motivation:	"Don't let people pull you into their storm. Pull them into your peace." – Kimberly Jones
Battle's Bullet:	Boring is good. – This doesn't refer to boredom but an absence of adversity.

Personal Observances:
_____
_____
_____

January  24

Stand Firm

Inspiration: Psalm 33:11 - But the plans of the Lord **stand firm** forever, the purposes of his heart through all generations.

National Day: National Compliment Day

Anniversary: 1848 – Gold is discovered at Sutter's Mill in California

Born Today: 1918 – Oral Roberts - evangelist

Motivation: "When you reach the end of your rope, tie a knot in it and hang on." – President Thomas Jefferson

Battle's Bullet: If you don't receive the fruit of your labor immediately, do not become discouraged, but stay the course.

Personal Observances:
_____
_____
_____

January 25

Wisdom

Inspiration:	**Proverbs 1:7 - The fear of the Lord is the beginning of** Knowledge, but fools despise **wisdom** and instruction.
National Day:	National Opposites Day
Anniversary:	1819 – University of Virginia is chartered, Thomas Jefferson a founder
Born Today:	1981 – Alicia Keys - music
Motivation:	"It is not what you look at that matters, it is what you see." – Henry David Thoreau
Battle's Bullet:	There is NO individual liberty without political **and** economic freedom.

Personal Observances:

_____
_____
_____

January 26

Perseverance

Inspiration:	**Romans 5:3** - Not only so, but we also glory in our sufferings, because we know that suffering produces **perseverance**; **perseverance**, character; and character, hope.
National Day:	National Spouses Day
Anniversary:	1871 – U.S. income tax is repealed
Born Today:	1917 – Louis Zamperini – Olympic athlete and military
Motivation:	"Never let the odds keep you from doing what you know in your heart you were meant to do." – H. Jackson Brown Jr.
Battle's Bullet:	It's not where we start in life that counts, but where we finish.

Personal Observances:
_____
_____
_____

January 27

Trustworthy - Trust

Inspiration: **Psalm 19:7** - The law of the Lord is perfect, refreshing the soul. The statutes of the Lord are **trustworthy**, making wise the simple.

National Day: National Chocolate Cake Day

Anniversary: 1956 – *Heartbreak Hotel* is released and becomes first hit for Elvis Presley

Born Today: 1955 – John G. Roberts Jr. – Chief Justice, U. S. Supreme Court

Motivation: "To be trusted is a greater compliment than being loved." – George MacDonald

Battle's Bullet: People value honesty over anything else in a relationship.

Personal Observances:
___
___
___

January 28

Truth

Inspiration: John 14:6 - Jesus answered, "I am the way and the **truth** and the life. No one comes to the Father except through me.

National Day: National Plan for a Vacation Day

Anniversary: 1878 – First telephone exchange opens in New Haven, Connecticut

Born Today: 1954 – Rick Warren – evangelical pastor

Motivation: "If you tell the truth, it becomes part of your past. If you lie, it becomes part of your future." – unknown

Battle's Bullet: What we do today, tomorrow, and the rest of our tomorrow's is more important than what we did yesterday.

Personal Observances:
___
___
___

January 29

Victorious

Inspiration: **Psalm 45:4** - In your majesty ride forth **victorious**ly in the cause of truth, humility and justice; let your right hand achieve awesome deeds.

National Day: National Puzzle Day

Anniversary: 1845 – *The Raven* is first published by author, Edgar Allen Poe

Born Today: 1843 – President William McKinley (25)

Motivation: "There is something in you that the world needs." – Lifehack

Battle's Bullet: He who defines the debate wins the argument.

Personal Observances:
_____
_____
_____

January 30

Thankful

Inspiration: **Philippians 4:6** - Do not be anxious about anything, but in every situation, by prayer and petition, with **thanksgiving**, present your requests to God.

National Day: National Croissant Day

Anniversary: 1971 – UCLA begins 88 game basketball winning streak

Born Today: 1882 – President Franklin D. Roosevelt (32)

Motivation: "There is always something to be thankful for." – Unknown

Battle's Bullet: Longing for what we want in the future obscures our appreciation for what we have in the present.

Personal Observances:
_____
_____
_____

January  31

Good Cheer

Inspiration: **Proverbs 12:25** - Anxiety weighs down the heart, but a kind word **cheer**s it up.

National Day: National Hot Chocolate Day

Anniversary: 1934 – President Roosevelt de-values gold to $ 35 per ounce where it stayed until 1971 when President Nixon took the country off of the gold standard.

Born Today: 1919 – Jackie Robinson - baseball

Motivation: "Your love of liberty, your respect for the laws, your habits of industry, and your practice of moral and religious obligations, are the strongest claims to national and individual happiness." – President George Washington

Battle's Bullet: Have a sense of humor. Things are never as bad as they may appear. A sense of humor will lighten most situations.

Personal Observances:
_____
_____
_____

FEBRUARY

FEBRUARY 1

Joy

Inspiration:	**Psalm 16:11** - You make known to me the path of life; you will fill me with **joy** in your presence, with eternal pleasures at your right hand.
National Day:	National Freedom Day
Anniversary:	1898 – Travelers issues the first auto insurance policy
Born Today:	1894 – John Ford – movie director
Motivation:	"Joy is the echo of God's lite in us." – Unknown
Battle's Bullet:	It is a joy to know that you have been a small instrument to help someone's life.

Personal Observances:

_____
_____
_____

February 2

Honor

Inspiration:	**Proverbs 21:21** - Whoever pursues righteousness and love finds life, prosperity and **honor**.
National Day:	Groundhog Day
Anniversary:	1887 – First Groundhog Day observed in Punxsutawney, Pennsylvania
Born Today:	1905 – Ayn Rand - author
Motivation:	"There is no limit to the amount of good you can do if you don't care who gets the credit." – President Ronald Reagan
Battle's Bullet:	What you do in the present will create a past that will greatly influence your opportunities and dreams in the future.

Personal Observances:
_____
_____
_____

LIFE'S DAILY TREASURE

February  3

Heart

Inspiration: **Jeremiah 29:13** - You will seek me and find me when you seek me with all your **heart**.

National Day: National Missing Persons Day

Anniversary: 1863 – Samuel Clemens first becomes Mark Twain writing for *The Territorial Enterprise* in Nevada

Born Today: 1894 – Norman Rockwell - illustrator

Motivation: "A kind heart is a fountain of gladness, making everything in its vicinity freshen into smiles." – Washington Irving

Battle's Bullet: Do not lose heart when you find obstacles in your path. That is the time to bear down.

Personal Observances:
_____
_____
_____

February 4

Hope

Inspiration: **Psalm 130:5** - I wait for the Lord, my whole being waits, and in his word I put my **hope**.

National Day: National Thank a Mail Carrier Day

Anniversary: 1887 – Interstate Commerce Act is passed to regulate railroads

Born Today: 1902 – Charles Lindbergh

Motivation: "Once you choose hope, everything's possible." – Christopher Reeve

Battle's Bullet: As long as you have Hope, things can always be worse.

Personal Observances:
_____
_____
_____

FEBRUARY 5

Courage

Inspiration: **Deuteronomy 31:6** - Be strong and **courage**ous. Do not be afraid or terrified because of them, for the Lord your God goes with you; he will never leave you nor forsake you."

National Day: National Weatherperson's Day

Anniversary: 1850 – Adding machine using depressible keys in patented in New York

Born Today: 1837 – Dwight L. Moody

Motivation: "He who refuses to embrace a unique opportunity loses the prize as surely as if he had failed." – William James

Battle's Bullet: Confidence precedes commitment and then action to success.

Personal Observances:
_____
_____
_____

February 6

Act

Inspiration:	**1 John 3:18** - Dear children, let us not love with words or speech but with **act**ions and in truth.
National Day:	National Frozen Yogurt Day
Anniversary:	1935 – Monopoly board game debuts
Born Today:	1911 – President Ronald Reagan (40) 1895 – Babe Ruth
Motivation:	"Don't judge each day by the harvest you reap, but by the seeds that you plant." – Robert Louis Stevenson
Battle's Bullet:	We can't do anything positive with a negative attitude.

Personal Observances:
___
___
___

LIFE'S DAILY TREASURE

February 7

Fearless

Inspiration:	**Psalm 27:3** - Though an army besiege me, my heart will **not fear**; though war break out against me, even then I will be confident.
National Day:	National Send a Card to a Friend Day
Anniversary:	1940 – Walt Disney premieres *Pinocchio* film
Born Today:	1867 – Laura Ingalls Wilder 1919 – Desmond Doss
Motivation:	"Worry does not empty tomorrow of its sorrow, it empties today of its strength." – Corrie Ten Boom
Battle's Bullet:	Please give me the fearlessness of my youth to achieve the dreams of my adulthood.

Personal Observances:

_____
_____
_____

February 8

Humble

Inspiration: **Psalm 18:27** -You save the **humble** but bring low those whose eyes are haughty.

National Day: National Boy Scouts Day

Anniversary: 1910 – The Boy Scouts of America is incorporated

Born Today: 1932 – John Williams – composer and conductor

Motivation: Humility is the mother of giants. One sees great things from the valley; only small things from the peak." – G. K. Chesterton

Battle's Bullet: Be humble. As the saying goes, "There hasn't ever been a horse that can't be rode, and there's never been a rider that can't be throwed."

Personal Observances:
_____
_____
_____

FEBRUARY 9

Faith - Faithful

Inspiration:	**Psalm 33:4** - For the word of the Lord is right and true; he is **faith**ful in all he does.
National Day:	National Pizza Day
Anniversary:	1825 – U. S. House of Representatives elects John Quincy Adams president
Born Today:	1773 – President William Henry Harrison (9) 1737 – Thomas Paine
Motivation:	"Faith is taking the first step even when you don't see the entire staircase." – Martin Luther King Jr.
Battle's Bullet:	Our faith is only beneficial if placed in the right place.

Personal Observances:

_____
_____
_____

February 10

Provision

Inspiration: **1 Corinthians 10:13** - No temptation has overtaken you except what is common to mankind. And God is faithful; he will not let you be tempted beyond what you can bear. But when you are tempted, he will also **provide** a way out so that you can endure it.

National Day: National Umbrella Day

Anniversary: 1933 – Delivery of the first singing telegram in New York City

Born Today: 1930 – Robert Wagner – actor

Motivation: "God's path will never lack God's provision." – Tony Evans

Battle's Bullet: We have the choice when adversity arrives to get closer to God for His grace, comfort, and provision, or move further away from Him.

Personal Observances:
___
___
___

February  11

Mercy

Inspiration: **Psalm 40:11** - Do not withhold your **mercy** from me, Lord; may your love and faithfulness always protect me.

National Day: National Shut-In Visitation Day

Anniversary: 1809 – Robert Fulton patents the steamboat

Born Today: 1847 – Thomas Edison

Motivation: "I have always found mercy bears richer fruits than strict justice." – President Abraham Lincoln

Battle's Bullet: Every day I am thankful for the mercy that I've received and strive to do something in His service.

Personal Observances:
_____
_____
_____

February 12

Forgiveness

Inspiration: **Psalm 25:11** - For the sake of your name, Lord, **forgive** my iniquity, though it is great.

National Day: National Plum Pudding Day

Anniversary: 1924 – George Gershwin premieres *Rhapsody in Blue* in New York

Born Today: 1809 – President Abraham Lincoln (16)

Motivation: "Forgiveness does not change the past but it does enlarge the future." – Paul Lewis Boese

Battle's Bullet: Feelings of anger and envy don't hurt the other person half as much as they hurt us because they prevent us from focusing and achieving positive results.

Personal Observances:
_____
_____
_____

February 13

Grace

Inspiration:	**Ephesians 2:8-9** - For it is by **grace** you have been saved, through faith—and this is not from yourselves, it is the gift of God—not by works, so that no one can boast.
National Day:	National Cheddar Day
Anniversary:	1866 – Jesse James holds up his first bank located in Missouri
Born Today:	1922 – Hal Moore - military
Motivation:	"God's mercy and Grace give me hope, for myself and our world." – Billy Graham
Battle's Bullet:	God's Grace has been and is always bigger than my need.

Personal Observances:

_____
_____
_____

February 14

Love

Inspiration:	1 Corinthians 13:4, 6, 8, 13 - **Love** is patient, **love** is kind. It does not envy, it does not boast, it is not proud. **Love** does not delight in evil but rejoices with the truth. **Love** never fails. And now these three remain: faith, hope and **love**. But the greatest of these is **love**.
National Day:	Valentine's Day
Anniversary:	1803 – Supreme Court Chief Justice John Marshall declares any laws passed by Congress that conflicts with the Constitution are unconstitutional
Born Today:	1818 – Frederick Douglas
Motivation:	"Though our feelings come and go, God's love for us does not." – C. S. Lewis
Battle's Bullet:	God has loved me more than I deserve, provided me all I have needed, and carried me when I could not walk.

Personal Observances:

_____
_____
_____

February  15

Rejoice

Inspiration:	Philippians 4:4-9 - **Rejoice** in the Lord always. I will say it again: **Rejoice**! Let your gentleness be evident to all. The Lord is near. Do not be anxious about anything, but in every situation, by prayer and petition, with thanksgiving, present your requests to God...
National Day:	Singles Awareness Day
Anniversary:	1898 – U.S.S. Maine sunk in Havana harbor with the loss of 298 precipitating the Spanish-American War
Born Today:	1803 – John Sutter
Motivation:	"Despite the conditions of our day, we have many reasons to rejoice and be optimistic." – Bonnie L. Oscarson
Battle's Bullet:	I put my trust in the palm of the Lord's hand.

Personal Observances:

_____
_____
_____

February 16

Adversity – Trials - Obstacles

Inspiration: **James 1:2-4** - Consider it pure joy, my brothers and sisters, whenever you face **trials** of many kinds, because you know that the testing of your faith produces perseverance. Let perseverance finish its work so that you may be mature and complete, not lacking anything.

National Day: National Do a Grouch a Favor Day

Anniversary: 1932 – First patent issued for a peach tree

Born Today: 1884 – Robert Flaherty – explorer, called father of documentary film

Motivation: "Out of adversity comes opportunity." – Benjamin Franklin

Battle's Bullet: Overcoming adversity through experience is a true gift.

Personal Observances:
_____
_____
_____

February 17

Encouragement

Inspiration: 1 Thessalonians 5:11 - Therefore **encourage** one another and build each other up, just as in fact you are doing.

National Day: National Random Acts of Kindness Day

Anniversary: 1801 – U. S. House of Representatives breaks electoral college tie to elect Thomas Jefferson

Born Today: 1889 – H. L. Hunt - oil

Motivation: "No one is useless in this world who lightens the burden of another." – Charles Dickens

Battle's Bullet: If we encourage at least one person per day, we'll have an enormous impact on the world.

Personal Observances:
_____
_____
_____

February 18

Endurance

Inspiration: 1 Timothy 6:11 - But you, man of God, flee from all this, and pursue righteousness, godliness, faith, love, **endurance** and gentleness.

National Day: National Drink Wine Day

Anniversary: 1885 – Mark Twain publishes *Huckleberry Finn*

Born Today: 1895 – George Gipp – "Win one for the Gipper" fame

Motivation: "If you remain calm in the midst of great chaos, it is the surest guarantee that it will eventually subside." – Julie Andrews

Battle's Bullet: Things are rarely as bad as they may appear to be at the moment.

Personal Observances:
___
___
___

February 19

Example

Inspiration:	**1 Corinthians 11:1** - Follow my **example**, as I follow the **example** of Christ.
National Day:	National Vet Girls RISE Day
Anniversary:	1878 – Thomas Edison receives a patent for the phonograph
Born Today:	1924 – Lee Marvin – actor/veteran
Motivation:	"The most powerful leadership tool you have is your own personal example." – Picturequotes.com
Battle's Bullet:	Everyone is an example to someone, and the best leadership is by example.

Personal Observances:

_____
_____
_____

February 20

Grow

Inspiration:	**Proverbs 20:13** - Do not love sleep or you will **grow** poor; stay awake and you will have food to spare.
National Day:	National Love Your Pet Day
Anniversary:	1962 – John Glenn is the first American to orbit Earth.
Born Today:	1902 – Ansel Adams - photographer
Motivation:	"It is **never** too late to be who you might have been." – George Elliot
Battle's Bullet:	Learn early, learn often, never stop learning. It will determine the level of your success.

Personal Observances:
_____
_____
_____

February 21

Overcomer

Inspiration:	**Matthew 16:18** - And I tell you that you are Peter, and on this rock I will build my church, and the gates of Hades will not **overcome** it.
National Day:	National Sticky Bun Day
Anniversary:	1947 – Edwin Land demonstrates the first instant developing camera.
Born Today:	1936 – Barbara Jordan –politician and educator
Motivation:	"Strength doesn't come from what you can do. It comes from overcoming the things you once thought you couldn't." – Unknown
Battle's Bullet:	Will we stop at the first sign of trouble, or will we stand and face it to succeed? If we quit, we may gain a momentary respite, but we will forgo the opportunity to overcome and learn from it.

Personal Observances:

_____
_____
_____

February 22

Patience

Inspiration: **Ecclesiastes 7:8** - The end of a matter is better than its beginning, and **patience** is better than pride.

National Day: National Margarita Day

Anniversary: 1942 – General MacArthur ordered to leave The Philippines and vows, "I shall return."

Born Today: 1732 – President George Washington (1)

Motivation: "Don't give up what you want most, for what you want now." – Unknown

Battle's Bullet: A dream delayed is not a dream denied.

Personal Observances:
___
___
___

February 23

Peace

Inspiration: **Proverbs 14:30** - A heart at **peace** gives life to the body, but envy rots the bones.

National Day: National Dog Biscuit Day

Anniversary: 1945 – U.S. Marines raise flag on Iwo Jima, which is immortalized in a picture.

Born Today: 1965 – Michael Dell, Dell Computers

Motivation: "When we are at peace on the inside, the troubles on the outside have little effect." – Michael P. Watson

Battle's Bullet: Don't listen to negativism. It is a cancer that will deter you from success.

Personal Observances:
_____
_____
_____

February 24

Stand Firm

Inspiration: 1 Corinthians 15:58 - Therefore, my dear brothers and sisters, **stand firm**. Let nothing move you. Always give yourselves fully to the work of the Lord, because you know that your labor in the Lord is not in vain.

National Day: National Tortilla Chip Day

Anniversary: 1942 – Battle of Los Angeles results in anti-aircraft fire for falsely rumored Japanese aircraft attacking the city.

Born Today: 1955 – Steve Jobs – founder of Apple

Motivation: "Be sure you put your feet in the right place, and then stand firm." – President Abraham Lincoln

Battle's Bullet: If you can't see a reward for all of your hard work, don't quit but be confident that your efforts will not be fruitless.

Personal Observances:
_____
_____
_____

February 25

Wisdom

Inspiration: **1 Kings 3:9** - So give your servant a **discerning heart** to govern your people and to distinguish between right and wrong.

National Day: National Clam Chowder Day

Anniversary: 1862 – Congress authorizes the first printing of U.S. notes.

Born Today: 1888 – John Foster Dulles – diplomat

Motivation: "You will never reach your destination if you stop and throw rocks at every dog that barks." – Winston Churchill

Battle's Bullet: Common sense is critical at any time, but more so in chaotic times.

Personal Observances:
___
___
___

February 26

Perseverance

Inspiration:	**2 Peter 1:6** - and to knowledge, self-control; and to self-control, **perseverance**; and to **perseverance** godliness
National Day:	National Tell a Fairy Tale Day
Anniversary:	1929 – President Calving Coolidge establishes Grand Teton National Park.
Born Today:	1846 – Buffalo Bill Cody
Motivation:	"Our greatest weakness lies in our giving up. The most certain way to succeed is always try just one more time." – Beinspiredchannel.com
Battle's Bullet:	We never reach our full potential until we fail at our highest achievement. Until then: Aim High, Work Hard, and NEVER Quit!

Personal Observances:

_____
_____
_____

February 27

Trustworthy - Trust

Inspiration: **Psalm 9:10** - Those who know your name **trust** in you, for you, Lord, have never forsaken those who seek you.

National Day: National Retro Day

Anniversary: 1801 – U.S. Congress assumes jurisdiction over Washington, D.C.

Born Today: 1932 – Elizabeth Taylor -actress

Motivation: "Live simply. Love generously, care deeply, speak kindly, leave the rest to God." – President Ronald Reagan

Battle's Bullet: When challenges arrive, we can grow closer to God or run further away. I'll move closer.

Personal Observances:
___
___
___

February 28

Truth

Inspiration:	**Romans 1:25** - They exchanged the **truth** about God for a lie, and worshiped and served created things rather than the Creator—who is forever praised. Amen.
National Day:	National Tooth Fairy Day
Anniversary:	1983 – Final episode of M.A.S.H. airs with a record television audience.
Born Today:	1923 – Charles Durning – actor/World War II veteran
Motivation:	"The truth is like a lion. You don't have to defend it. Let it loose. It will defend itself." – St. Augustine
Battle's Bullet:	Common sense is always in style and never goes out of season.

Personal Observances:

_____
_____
_____

February 29

Victorious

Inspiration: **Revelation 2:11** - Whoever has ears, let them hear what the Spirit says to the churches. The one who is **victorious** will not be hurt at all by the second death.

National Day: National Time Refund Day

Anniversary: 1940 – Hattie McDaniel becomes first African-American to win an Oscar for *Gone with The Wind*.

Born Today: 1904 – Jimmy Dorsey - music

Motivation: "He is no fool who gives what he can't keep to gain what he cannot lose." – Jim Elliot

Battle's Bullet: Achievement builds confidence, and confidence leads to more success.

Personal Observances:
___
___
___

MARCH

MARCH 1

Joy

Inspiration: **Romans 12:12** - Be **joy**ful in hope, patient in affliction, faithful in prayer.

National Day: National Peanut Butter Day

Anniversary: 1781 – Continental Congress adopts Articles of Confederation as first Constitution

Born Today: 1904 – Glenn Miller - music

Motivation: "Joy, the kind of happiness that doesn't depend on what happens." – David Steindl-Rast

Battle's Bullet: We experience ups and downs, swerve to the left and right, submit to discipline and freely have fun, and celebrate joy and endure heartaches as we traverse our life courses.

Personal Observances:
___
___
___

March  2

Honor

Inspiration:	**Hebrews 5:4** - And no one takes this **honor** on himself, but he receives it when called by God, just as Aaron was.
National Day:	National Old Stuff Day
Anniversary:	1836 – Texas Independence Day – Republic of Texas
Born Today:	1793 – Sam Houston – Texas and United States Statesman
Motivation:	"If honor were profitable, everybody would be honorable." – Thomas More
Battle's Bullet:	God helps us overcome troubles, and He honors our praise.

Personal Observances:

_____
_____
_____

March 3

Heart

Inspiration:	**Deuteronomy 6:5** - Love the Lord your God with all your **heart** and with all your soul and with all your strength.
National Day:	National Anthem Day
Anniversary:	1837 – U.S. Congress increases Supreme Court membership to 9 from 7.
Born Today:	1847 – Alexander Graham Bell - inventor
Motivation:	"When my heart is overwhelmed lead me to the rock that is higher than I." – King David
Battle's Bullet:	We should always be considerate of others with our actions.

Personal Observances:

_____
_____
_____

March 4

Hope

Inspiration:	Isaiah 40:31 - but those who **hope** in the Lord will renew their strength. They will soar on wings like eagles; they will run and not grow weary, they will walk and not be faint.
National Day:	National Hug a GI Day
Anniversary:	1933 – Franklin Roosevelt is last president inaugurated on this date before it was moved to January 20th by the 20th amendment to the Constitution.
Born Today:	1888 – Knute Rockne - football
Motivation:	"Learn from yesterday, live for today, hope for tomorrow." – Albert Einstein
Battle's Bullet:	ALWAYS have a positive attitude. There is always hope!

Personal Observances:

_____
_____
_____

March 5

Courage

Inspiration: **Joshua 1:9** - Have I not commanded you? Be strong and **courage**ous. Do not be afraid; do not be discouraged, for the Lord your God will be with you wherever you go.

National Day: National Multiple Personality Day

Anniversary: 1946 – Winston Churchill delivers "Iron Curtain" speech in Fulton, Missouri

Born Today: 1836 – Charles Goodnight - cattleman

Motivation: "Courage is not having the strength to go on. It is going on when you don't have the strength." – Theodore Roosevelt

Battle's Bullet: Don't look back; we're not going that way.

Personal Observances:

_____
_____
_____

MARCH  6

Act

Inspiration:	**Proverbs 13:16** - All who are prudent **act** with knowledge, but fools expose their folly.
National Day:	National Oreo Cookie Day
Anniversary:	1836 – The Alamo falls after a 13-day siege
Born Today:	1905 – Bob Wills - music
Motivation:	"Action speaks louder than words, but not nearly as often." – Mark Twain
Battle's Bullet:	If we base all of our decisions and actions on achieving the long-term reputation, we desire, we will be more successful.

Personal Observances:

_____
_____
_____

March 7

Fearless

Inspiration: 1 John 4:18 - There is no **fear** in love. But perfect love drives out **fear**, because **fear** has to do with punishment. The one who **fear**s is **not** made perfect in love.

National Day: National Flapjack Day

Anniversary: 1876 – Alexander Graham Bell patents the telephone

Born Today: 1849 – Luther Burbank – plant breeder

Motivation: "Worry is interest paid on trouble before it is due." –Lucille Braden

Battle's Bullet: The key to maximizing our decision success for today and to make decisions to stand the test of time is to get out of the present vacuum and consider past events and the impact on the future.

Personal Observances:

March 8

Humble

Inspiration:	**Ephesians 4:2** - Be completely **humble** and gentle; be patient, bearing with one another in love.
National Day:	International Women's Day
Anniversary:	1946 – First helicopter is licensed for commercial use in New York.
Born Today:	1841 – Oliver Wendell Holmes Jr. – U.S. Supreme Court
Motivation:	"The humble man makes room for progress; the proud man believes he is already there." – Ed Parker
Battle's Bullet:	It is my daily desire to receive the grace that God gives me and to live a life worthy of it.

Personal Observances:

_____
_____
_____

March  9

Faith - Faithful

Inspiration: **Psalm 86:11** - Teach me your way, Lord, that I may rely on your **faith**fulness; give me an undivided heart, that I may fear your name.

National Day: National Barbie Day

Anniversary: 1862 – USS Monitor and CSS Merrimack are first ironclad ships to fight each other.

Born Today: 1824 – Leland Stanford – founder of Stanford University

Motivation: "Sometimes life is gonna hit you in the head with a brick. Don't lose faith." – Steve Jobs

Battle's Bullet: God is in control and has a plan. Have Faith!

Personal Observances:
_____
_____
_____

March  10

Provision

Inspiration: Job 5:10 - He **provide**s rain for the earth; he sends water on the countryside.

National Day: National Pack Your Lunch Day

Anniversary: 1876 – First telephone call where Bell asks Watson to "come here"

Born Today: 1903 – Clare Booth Luce – playwright and politician

Motivation: "God has it all figured out. He will make a way where you don't see a way." – Spiritual Inspiration

Battle's Bullet: I know and experience reminders that the most successful endeavors of my life all occurred because of God's provision.

Personal Observances:
_____
_____
_____

March 11

Mercy

Inspiration:	**Zechariah 7:9** - "This is what the Lord Almighty said: 'Administer true justice; show **mercy** and compassion to one another.
National Day:	National Funeral and Mortician Recognition Day
Anniversary:	1918 – Spanish Flu epidemic claims its first U.S. victim
Born Today:	1936 – Antonin Scalia – U.S. Supreme Court
Motivation:	"All the great things are simple, and many can be expressed in a single word: freedom, justice, honor, duty, mercy, hope." – Winston Churchill
Battle's Bullet:	Despite this world's brokenness, more charity, culture, and grace have resulted in our country than with any society previously.

Personal Observances:
___
___
___

March  12

Forgiveness

Inspiration: Matthew 6:14-15 - For if you **forgive** other people when they sin against you, your heavenly Father will also **forgive** you. But if you do not **forgive** others their sins, your Father will not **forgive** your sins.

National Day: National Girl Scout Day

Anniversary: 1894 – Coca Cola is first sold in bottles

Born Today: 1946 – Liza Minnelli - entertainer

Motivation: "To forgive is to set a prisoner free and discover that the prisoner was you." – Lewis B. Smedes

Battle's Bullet: When we admit our mistakes, people will usually forgive us.

Personal Observances:
_____
_____
_____

March 13

Grace

Inspiration:	**2 Corinthians 12:9** - But he said to me, "My **grace** is sufficient for you, for my power is made perfect in weakness." Therefore, I will boast all the more gladly about my weaknesses, so that Christ's power may rest on me.
National Day:	National Good Samaritan Day
Anniversary:	1956 – *The Searchers* classic western film is released
Born Today:	1914 – Edwin "Butch" O'Hare – U.S. Navy – O'Hare airport in Chicago
Motivation:	"In God's garden of Grace, even a broken tree can bear fruit." – Rick Warren
Battle's Bullet:	Each of us were gifted unique gifts that enable us to excel at some things.

Personal Observances:

_____

_____

_____

March  14

Love

Inspiration:	**John 15:13** - Greater **love** has no one than this: to lay down one's life for one's friends.
National Day:	National Write Down Your Story Day
Anniversary:	1794 – Eli Whitney patents the cotton gin
Born Today:	1879 – Albert Einstein - inventor
Motivation:	"He loves us not because we are all lovable, but because He is love." – wordsonimages.com
Battle's Bullet:	Relationships are the essential thing in life.

Personal Observances:
_____
_____
_____

March 15

Rejoice

Inspiration: 1 Peter 4:13 - But **rejoice** in as much as you participate in the sufferings of Christ, so that you may be overjoyed when his glory is revealed.

National Day: National Everything You Think is Wrong Day

Anniversary: 1869 – Cincinnati Red Stockings (now Reds) become the first professional baseball team.

Born Today: 1767 – President Andrew Jackson (7)

Motivation: "Rejoice not in another man's misfortune." – Pythagoras

Battle's Bullet: Isn't it interesting that we live in a country that celebrates individual freedom, but others often scorn us if we exercise our liberty and don't follow the crowd?

Personal Observances:
_____
_____
_____

March  16

Adversity – Trials - Obstacles

Inspiration: Psalm 9:9 - The LORD is a refuge for the oppressed, a stronghold in times of trouble.

National Day: National Everything You Think is Right Day

Anniversary: 1802 – U. S. Military Academy at West Point, N.Y. is Founded.

Born Today: 1751 – President James Madison (4)

Motivation: "We don't grow when things are easy. We grow when we face challenges." - Unknown

Battle's Bullet: In adversity, I learned not to ask "why me" but "what now" in the hope I would only suffer once to learn my intended lesson. It has served me repeatedly and very well.

Personal Observances:
___
___
___

MARCH 17

Encouragement

Inspiration: **2 Timothy 4:2** - Preach the word; be prepared in season and out of season; correct, rebuke and **encourage**—with great patience and careful instruction.

National Day: St. Patrick's Day

Anniversary: 1898 – John Phillip Holland successfully tests first modern submarine

Born Today: 1902 – Bobby Jones – golf

Motivation: "Don't live in the past thinking about mistakes or changes you made. Think of your life as a book, move forward, close one chapter and open another. Learn from your mistakes but focus on your future, not on your past." – Unknown

Battle's Bullet: I look daily for opportunities to encourage others.

Personal Observances:
_____
_____
_____

March 18

Endurance

Inspiration: **Colossians 1:11** - being strengthened with all power according to his glorious might so that you may have great **endurance** and patience

National Day: National Supreme Sacrifice Day

Anniversary: 1881 – Barnum and Bailey circus debuts in Madison Square Garden. Runs 146 years.

Born Today: 1837 – President Grover Cleveland (22 and 24)

Motivation: "Endurance is not just the ability to bear a hard thing, but to turn it into glory." – William Barclay

Battle's Bullet: As I grow nearer to the end of my course, my focus is ever greater to utilize each day on my path wisely to return the favors I received to others.

Personal Observances:
_____
_____
_____

March 19

Example

Inspiration: 1 Peter 2:21 - To this you were called, because Christ suffered for you, leaving you an **example**, that you should follow in his steps.

National Day: National Let's Laugh Day

Anniversary: 2003 – Invasion of Iraq begins as part of war on terror

Born Today: 1590 – William Bradford, Mayflower

1848 – Wyatt Earp

Motivation: "You are an example. Whether you are a good example or not is up to you." – Steve Ferrante

Battle's Bullet: Everything we do today will impact our future and those we touch.

Personal Observances:

_____
_____
_____

March 20

Grow

Inspiration: **Hebrews 12:15** - See to it that no one falls short of the grace of God and that no bitter root **grow**s up to cause trouble and defile many.

National Day: National Proposal Day

Anniversary: 1852 – *Uncle Tom's Cabin* by Harriet Beecher Stowe is published

Born Today: 1928 – Fred Rogers - television

Motivation: "Personal growth is not a matter of learning new information but of unlearning old limits." – Alan Cohen

Battle's Bullet: Failure to step out of our comfort zone to achieve something significant puts us at 100% risk of never growing beyond where we are now.

Personal Observances:
_____
_____
_____

March 21

Overcomer

Inspiration: **Romans 12:21** - Do not be **overcome** by evil, but **overcome** evil with good.

National Day: National Single Parent Day

Anniversary: 1963 – Alcatraz prison closes

Born Today: 1856 – Henry Ossian Flipper – former slave, first African-American West Point graduate

Motivation: "Although the world is full of suffering, it is also full of the overcoming it." – Helen Keller

Battle's Bullet: The "easy way out" is usually only easy in the short run.

Personal Observances:
_____
_____
_____

March  22

Patience

Inspiration: **Colossians 3:12** - Therefore, as God's chosen people, holy and dearly loved, clothe yourselves with compassion, kindness, humility, gentleness and **patience**.

National Day: National Goof Off Day

Anniversary: 1960 – First patent issued for lasers

Born Today: 1908 – Louis L'Amour – author

Motivation: "Someday you'll look back and understand why it all happened the way it did." – notsalmon.com

Battle's Bullet: Patience is often painfully learned from experience.

Personal Observances:
___
___
___

March 23

Peace

Inspiration:	**Hebrews 12:11** - No discipline seems pleasant at the time, but painful. Later on, however, it produces a harvest of righteousness and **peace** for those who have been trained by it.
National Day:	National Puppy Day
Anniversary:	1775 – Patrick Henry declares "Give me liberty or give me death" in a speech.
Born Today:	1900 – Eric Fromm philosopher
Motivation:	"There is no greater wealth in this world than peace of mind." – Unknown
Battle's Bullet:	No government is powerful enough to rely on for peace and safety.

Personal Observances:

_____
_____
_____

March  24

Stand Firm

Inspiration: 1 Peter 5:9 - Resist him, **stand**ing **firm** in the faith, because you know that the family of believers throughout the world is undergoing the same kind of sufferings.

National Day: National Cheesesteak Day

Anniversary: 1664 – Roger Williams is granted a charter to colonize Rhode Island

Born Today: 1930 – Steve McQueen - actor

Motivation: "Stay positive, stay fighting, stay brave, stay ambitious, stay focused, stay strong." – inspirational picturequotes.com

Battle's Bullet: We stand on the shoulders of the nation's founders, our forefathers, and others who went before us who gave us this republic we enjoy.

Personal Observances:
_____
_____
_____

March 25

Wisdom

Inspiration: **James 1:5** - If any of you lacks **wisdom**, you should ask God, who gives generously to all without finding fault, and it will be given to you.

National Day: National Medal of Honor Day

Anniversary: 1954 – First color television set manufactured by RCA

Born Today: 1928 – Jim Lovell - astronaut

Motivation: "A leader's trustworthiness is the sum of his or her daily actions." – Jennifer V. Miller

Battle's Bullet: Striving for consensus is not leadership.

Personal Observances:
___
___
___

March 26

Perseverance

Inspiration: **Galatians 6:9** - Let us not become weary in doing good, for at the proper time we will reap a harvest if we do not give up.

National Day: Epilepsy Awareness Day – Purple Day

Anniversary: 1955 – *Ballad of Davy Crockett* becomes #1 record in U.S

Born Today: 1874 – Robert Frost - poet

Motivation: "A person who falls and gets back up is much stronger than a person who never fell." – Roy T. Bennett

Battle's Bullet: The longer our time perspective, the smaller today's problems appear. The shorter our perspective, the larger they appear.

Personal Observances:
_____
_____
_____

March 27

Trustworthy - Trust

Inspiration: **Psalm 28:7** - The Lord is my strength and my shield; my heart **trust**s in him, and he helps me. My heart leaps for joy, and with my song I praise him.

National Day: National Scribble Day

Anniversary: 1855 – Kerosene is patented by Abraham Gesner

Born Today: 1963 – Quentin Tarantino – director and screenwriter

Motivation: "To be trusted is a greater compliment than to be loved." – lifehacks.io

Battle's Bullet: Treat other people's money as you would your own. If only politicians learned this truth.

Personal Observances:
_____
_____
_____

March  28

Truth

Inspiration:	3 John 4 - I have no greater joy than to hear that my children are walking in the truth.
National Day:	National Something on a Stick Day
Anniversary:	1935 – Patent for gyroscope for rockets is patented by Robert Goddard
Born Today:	1955 – Reba McEntire – singer and actress
Motivation:	"Truth will always be truth, regardless of lack of understanding, disbelief or ignorance." – W. Clement Stone
Battle's Bullet:	There are two types of people. Some people look for ways to make things happen, and others look for reasons why they can't occur. They both achieve what they see.

Personal Observances:
_____
_____
_____

March 29

Victorious

Inspiration: **1 Corinthians 15:54-57** - When the perishable has been clothed with the imperishable, and the mortal with immortality, then the saying that is written will come true: "Death has been swallowed up in victory." "Where, O death, is your victory? Where, O death, is your sting?"

National Day: National Mom and Pop Business Day

Anniversary: 1848 – Niagara Falls stops flowing due to an ice jam

Born Today: 1790 – President John Tyler (10)

Motivation: "They might not like you, but they can't stop you. Keep working!" – explorepic.com

Battle's Bullet: Choice+ Chance+ Change+ Channel+ Commitment+ Consistent+ Come Again = Champion

Personal Observances:
___
___
___

March  30

Thankful

Inspiration: 1 Timothy 4:4 - For everything God created is good, and nothing is to be rejected if it is received with thanksgiving

National Day: National Doctors Day

Anniversary: 1867 – U. S. buys Alaska from Russia for about 2 cents per acre

Born Today: 1913 – Frankie Laine – singer

Motivation: "Be thankful for what you have. Your life, no matter how bad you think it is, is someone else's fairytale." - Wale Ayeni

Battle's Bullet: I'm not in control of much, if anything. Thankfully, God is always in control.

Personal Observances:
_____
_____
_____

MARCH 31

Good Cheer

Inspiration: **2 Corinthians 9:7** - Each of you should give what you have decided in your heart to give, not reluctantly or under compulsion, for God loves a **cheer**ful giver.

National Day: National Prom Day

Anniversary: 1918 – First daylight savings time in U.S. becomes effective

Born Today: * - Tecumseh (exact date unknown)

Motivation: "Being happy doesn't mean everything is perfect. It means you've decided to look beyond the imperfections." - thedailyquotes.com

Battle's Bullet: Make friends with as many people as possible. Those relationships are the most essential thing in life, next to our relationship with God and our family. If we have friends and are a true friend in return, we will have a wide range of opportunities during our life.

Personal Observances:
___
___
___

APRIL

April 1

Joy

Inspiration: **Psalm 92:4** - For you make me glad by your deeds, Lord; I sing for **joy** at what your hands have done.

National Day: April Fool's Day

Anniversary: 1976 – Apple Computer founded by Steve Wozniak and Steve Jobs

Born Today: 1901 – Whitaker Chambers - journalist

Motivation: "Happiness is smiling when the sun's out. Joy is dancing in the downpour." – Rend Collective

Battle's Bullet: Every day is a gift that passes and will not return. It is our choice to cherish it or to waste it with disrespect.

Personal Observances:
_____
_____
_____

April  2

Honor

Inspiration: **Proverbs 22:4** - Humility is the fear of the Lord; its wages are riches and **honor** and life.

National Day: National Peanut Butter and Jelly Day

Anniversary: 1917 – Republican Jeannette Rankin from Montana is the first woman member of the U.S. House of Representatives.

Born Today: 1939 – Marvin Gaye - singer

Motivation: "A hundred years cannot replace a moment's lost honor." – Proverb

Battle's Bullet: Live for others and honor God. Serving the needs of others is gratifying and is commended by God.

Personal Observances:
_____
_____
_____

April 3

Heart

Inspiration: Matthew 11:29 - Take my yoke upon you and learn from me, for I am gentle and humble in **heart**, and you will find rest for your souls.

National Day: National Find a Rainbow Day

Anniversary: 1882 – Jesse James is killed at home by Bob Ford

Born Today: 1783 – Washington Irving – author

Motivation: "Prayer is the best weapon we possess. It is the key that opens the heart of God." – San Pio De Pietrelcina

Battle's Bullet: We should honor and learn from the past, live and contribute in the present, hope and prepare for the future.

Personal Observances:
___
___
___

April  4

Hope

Inspiration:	**Easter (date varies)** - <u>Luke 24:6</u> - **He is not he**re; **he** has risen! Remember how **he** told you, while **he** was still with you in Galilee
National Day:	National School Librarian Day
Anniversary:	1968 – Martin Luther King Jr. is assassinated
Born Today:	1899 – Gloria Swanson - actress
Motivation:	"Hope is activated when we can say to ourselves: "I am willing to trust, wait without demanding answers, and to contribute myself to the most positive use of the present." – aimhappy.com
Battle's Bullet:	Forget yesterday, enjoy today, hope for tomorrow

Personal Observances:
___
___
___

April 5

Courage

Inspiration: **Acts 27:25** - So keep up your **courage**, men, for I have faith in God that it will happen just as he told me.

National Day: Gold Star Spouses Day

Anniversary: 1923 – Firestone Tire begins producing inflatable tires

Born Today: 1856 – Booker T. Washington - educator

Motivation: "Courage is being scared and saddling up anyway." - John Wayne

Battle's Bullet: Will we have the courage to take risks and step into unfamiliar ground to achieve significant success?

Personal Observances:
_____
_____
_____

April 6

Act

Inspiration:	**Psalm 106:2** - Who can proclaim the mighty **act**s of the Lord or fully declare his praise?
National Day:	National Student-Athletes Day
Anniversary:	1889 – Kodak begins selling rolled film
Born Today:	1937 – Merle Haggard - music
Motivation:	"Whenever you do a thing, act as if the whole world were watching." – President Thomas Jefferson
Battle's Bullet:	We must always think before we act. Something done is much harder to undo than do differently.

Personal Observances:
_____
_____
_____

April 7

Fearless

Inspiration: **Psalm 46:2** - Therefore we will **not fear**, though the earth give way and the mountains fall into the heart of the sea

National Day: National No Housework Day

Anniversary: 1805 – Lewis and Clark begin expedition to the Pacific Ocean

Born Today: 1928 – James Garner - actor

Motivation: "Do the thing you fear most and the death of fear is certain." – Mark Twain

Battle's Bullet: Things are rarely as bad as we fear.

Personal Observances:

_____
_____
_____

April  8

Humble

Inspiration:	**Psalm 149:4** - For the Lord takes delight in his people; he crowns the **humble** with victory.
National Day:	National Zoo Lovers Day
Anniversary:	1913 – 17th amendment to the U.S. Constitution is ratified providing for the direct election of U.S. Senators.
Born Today:	1974 – Chris Kyle - military
Motivation:	"Be humble, be teachable, and always keep learning." – Unknown
Battle's Bullet:	It doesn't matter how old we are or what position we hold in society. We influence others by our actions, whether they are positive or negative.

Personal Observances:
___
___
___

April 9

Faith - Faithful

Inspiration: **Psalm 40:11** - Do not withhold your mercy from me, Lord; may your love and **faith**fulness always protect me.

National Day: National Former Prisoners of War Recognition Day

Anniversary: 1865 – General Robert E. Lee surrenders his army at Appomattox Court House

Born Today: 1892 – Mary Pickford – actress

Motivation: "Faith is seeing light with your heart when all your eyes see is darkness." – Barbara Johnson

Battle's Bullet: My faith helps me endure setbacks knowing that the LORD will take better care of me than I deserve.

Personal Observances:
___
___
___

April 10

Provision

Inspiration:	**Job 10:12** - You gave me life and showed me kindness, and in your **provide**nce watched over my spirit.
National Day:	National Siblings Day
Anniversary:	1849 – Safety pin is patented in New York City
Born Today:	1827 – Lew Wallace – soldier, politician, author of *Ben-Hur*
Motivation:	"God will always provide. It just might look different than what we had in mind." – crosscards.com
Battle's Bullet:	While pop culture emphasizes enjoying the moment, if we desire anything above what government assistance provides, we are compelled to put leisure aside and work to earn what we want.

Personal Observances:
_____
_____
_____

April  11

Mercy

Inspiration:	**1 Peter 1:3** - Praise be to the God and Father of our Lord Jesus Christ! In his great **mercy** he has given us new birth into a living hope through the resurrection of Jesus Christ from the dead
National Day:	National Pet Day
Anniversary:	1899 – Treaty of Paris ends the Spanish-American War with Puerto Rico being ceded to the U.S
Born Today:	1899 – Percy Lavon Julius - chemist
Motivation:	"Our mind cannot find a comparison too large for expressing the superabundant mercy of the Lord toward his people." - David Dickson
Battle's Bullet:	There is no percentage of success in continually testing God's Grace and Mercy.

Personal Observances:

_____
_____
_____

April  12

Forgiveness

Inspiration: Luke 6:37 - "Do not judge, and you will not be judged. Do not condemn, and you will not be condemned. **Forgive**, and you will be **forgive**n.

National Day: National Grilled Cheese Sandwich Day

Anniversary: 1861 – Ft. Sumter is attacked by Confederates beginning the Civil War

Born Today: 1831 – Grenville Dodge - engineer

Motivation: "The weak can never forgive. Forgiveness is the attribute of the strong." – Mahatma Gandhi

Battle's Bullet: Be honest. ALWAYS tell the truth. People will forgive a mistake but will never trust a liar.

Personal Observances:
___
___
___

April  13

Grace

Inspiration:	**Ephesians 1:7** - In him we have redemption through his blood, the forgiveness of sins, in accordance with the riches of God's **grace**
National Day:	National Thomas Jefferson Day
Anniversary:	1860 – The first Pony Express rider reaches Sacramento
Born Today:	1743 – President Thomas Jefferson (3)
Motivation:	"The law condemns the best of us; but Grace saves the worst of us." – Joseph Prince
Battle's Bullet:	God's Grace is sufficient for every situation!

Personal Observances:

_____
_____
_____

April  14

Love

Inspiration: 1 Corinthians 2:9 -However, as it is written: "What no eye has seen, what no ear has heard, and what no human mind has conceived"— the things God has prepared for those who **love** him—

National Day: Look Up at the Sky Day

Anniversary: 1865 – President Abraham Lincoln is shot at Ford's Theater and dies the next day

Born Today: 1866 – Anne Sullivan Macy – educator of Helen Keller

Motivation: "The Christian does not think God will love us because we are good, but that God will make us good because He loves us." – C. S. Lewis

Battle's Bullet: Be confident your gifts to others will benefit many during and beyond your lifetime.

Personal Observances:

_____

_____

_____

April 15

Rejoice

Inspiration:	**Psalm 104:31** - May the glory of the Lord endure forever; may the Lord **rejoice** in his works—
National Day:	National Tax Day
Anniversary:	1955 – The first McDonald's restaurant is opened by Ray Kroc
Born Today:	1889 – Thomas Hart Benton - painter
Motivation:	"Rejoice in the things that are present; all else is beyond thee." – Michel De Montaigne
Battle's Bullet:	The person who is always looking to learn more, give more, pick up the slack wherever it may be, and do whatever job will help the team triumph will stand out like a full moon on a cloudless night.

Personal Observances:

_____
_____
_____

April  16

Adversity – Trials - Obstacles

Inspiration: **1 Peter 1:6** - In all this you greatly rejoice, though now for a little while you may have had to suffer grief in all kinds of **trial**s.

National Day: National Healthcare Decisions Day

Anniversary: 1926 – Book-of-the-Month club mails their inaugural offerings

Born Today: 1867 – Wilbur Wright – inventor and aviation

Motivation: "In life you'll have your back against the wall many times. You might as well get used to it." – Bear Bryant

Battle's Bullet: We will all face trials in life. How we respond, what we learn, and who we can help from the lessons are paramount.

Personal Observances:
_____
_____
_____

April  17

Encouragement

Inspiration: **Psalm 10:17** - You, Lord, hear the desire of the afflicted; you **encourage** them, and you listen to their cry,

National Day: National Ellis Island Family History Day

Anniversary: 1905 – U.S. Supreme Court judges the maximum 10-hour work day for bankers is unconstitutional

Born Today: 1837 – J. P. Morgan - financier

Motivation: "There is no exercise better for the heart than reaching down and lifting people up." – John Holmes

Battle's Bullet: Think of our country's great leaders, pioneers, inventors, and others who achieved great things after being encouraged in their efforts.

Personal Observances:

_____
_____
_____

April 18

Endurance

Inspiration:	1 Chronicles 16:34 - Give thanks to the LORD, for he is good; his love **endure**s forever.
National Day:	National Lineman Appreciation Day
Anniversary:	1942 – Doolittle Raiders bomb Japan in the first U.S. offensive action of World War II
Born Today:	1857 – Clarence Darrow - lawyer
Motivation:	"Don't pray for an easy life. Pray for the strength to endure a difficult one." – Bruce Lee
Battle's Bullet:	When we succumb to adversity, we miss the lessons and spirit to endure suffering until it abates.

Personal Observances:

_____
_____
_____

April  19

Example

Inspiration: **Titus 2:7** - In everything set them an **example** by doing what is good. In your teaching show integrity, seriousness

National Day: National Oklahoma City Bombing Appreciation Day

Anniversary: 1775 – The shot heard round the world at Lexington, Massachusetts after Paul Revere's and William Dawes' rides

Born Today: 1903 – Eliot Ness – crime fighter/Untouchables

Motivation: "Being a good example is the best form of service." – Sathya Sai Baba

Battle's Bullet: Will we set an example and ask others to follow it, or will we sit in an ivory tower and expect others to follow our words?

Personal Observances:
_____
_____
_____

April  20

Grow

Inspiration:	**2 Peter 3:18** - But **grow** in the grace and knowledge of our Lord and Savior Jesus Christ. To him be glory both now and forever! Amen.
National Day:	National Look Alike Day
Anniversary:	1912 – Fenway Park opens in Boston
Born Today:	1850 – David Chester French - sculptor
Motivation:	"The will of God will never lead you where the Grace of God will not protect you." – Winning Path
Battle's Bullet:	Don't let the person you are prevent you from becoming the person you're meant to become. Pursue your dreams!

Personal Observances:

_____
_____
_____

April 21

Overcomer

Inspiration: **Jeremiah 1:19** - They will fight against you but will not **overcome** you, for I am with you and will rescue you," declares the Lord.

National Day: National Kindergarten Day

Anniversary: 1836 – Texas wins its war for independence and becomes a Republic

Born Today: 1936 – James Dobson - evangelist

Motivation: "If you have overcome your inclination and not been overcome by it, you have reason to rejoice." --Plautus

Battle's Bullet: "Why me?" isn't the correct question when trouble comes, it is, "What lesson am I supposed to learn, and what now?"

Personal Observances:
_____
_____
_____

APRIL  22

Patience

Inspiration: Psalm 37:7 - Be still before the Lord and wait **patient**ly for him; do not fret when people succeed in their ways, when they carry out their wicked schemes.

National Day: National Girl Scouts Leaders' Day

Anniversary: 1864 – "In God We Trust" is first stamped on a 2-cent U.S. coin

Born Today: 1904- Robert Oppenheimer - physicist

Motivation: "Have patience with all things, but first of all with yourself." – Saint Francis de Sales

Battle's Bullet: Be patient. Nothing is free, and we have to pay dues to reap the rewards in life.

Personal Observances:
_____
_____
_____

April  23

Peace

Inspiration: **James 3:17** - But the wisdom that comes from heaven is first of all, pure; then **peace**-loving, considerate, submissive, full of mercy and good fruit, impartial and sincere.

National Day: National Picnic Day

Anniversary: 1985 – "New Coke" debuts; its failure is studied extensively

Born Today: 1791 – President James Buchanan (15)

Motivation: "You find peace not by rearranging the circumstances of your life, but by realizing who you are at the deepest level." – Eckhardt Tolle

Battle's Bullet: We don't grieve where our loved ones are but where they aren't.

Personal Observances:
___
___
___

April 24

Stand Firm

Inspiration:	**Psalm 119:89** - Your word, Lord, is eternal; it **stand**s **firm** in the heavens.
National Day:	National Pigs-In-A-Blanket Day
Anniversary:	1833 – First soda fountain is patented by Evert and Dulty
Born Today:	1940 – Sue Grafton - writer
Motivation:	"Give me a place to stand, and a lever long enough, and I will move the world." – Archimedes
Battle's Bullet:	Today, we stand on the threshold of unlimited opportunity. The world beckons, and we must choose whether we will leave this world without changing it or whether we will make a difference.

Personal Observances:
_____
_____
_____

April 25

Wisdom

Inspiration: **Proverbs 15:33 - Wisdom**'s instruction is to fear the Lord, and humility comes before honor.

National Day: National DNA Day

Anniversary: 1901 – New York is the first state to require automobile license plates

Born Today: 1908 – Edward R. Murrow - journalist

Motivation: "Wisdom is not the product of schooling but of the lifelong attempt to acquire it." – Albert Einstein

Battle's Bullet: Our Constitution's ideals, and the stability it has provided is unprecedented and priceless. Government by law is far superior to rule by men and women.

Personal Observances:
___
___
___

April 26

Perseverance

Inspiration: Hebrews 12:1 - Therefore, since we are surrounded by such a great cloud of witnesses, let us throw off everything that hinders and the sin that so easily entangles. And let us run with **perseverance** the race marked out for us,

National Day: National Kids and Pets Day

Anniversary: 1607 – Jamestown expedition makes their first landing in Virginia

Born Today: 1785 – John James Audubon - artist

Motivation: "For every obstacle there is a solution. Persistence is the key. The greatest mistake is giving up!" – President Dwight D. Eisenhower

Battle's Bullet: Anyone can do the things they like. Those who do the things they must do but don't want to will have more tremendous success than the majority.

Personal Observances:
_____
_____
_____

April 27

Trustworthy - Trust

Inspiration:	**Psalm 119:86** - All your commands are **trustworthy**; help me, for I am being persecuted without cause.
National Day:	National Tell a Story Day
Anniversary:	1805 – U. S. Marines land on the shores of Tripoli and attack the pirates
Born Today:	1822 – President Ulysses S. Grant (17)
	1791 – Samuel Morse - telegraph inventor
Motivation:	"Trustworthiness is shown in a person's actions, not just words." – therapy-talk.com
Battle's Bullet:	Is our reputation and trustworthiness essential to us? It is the companion to our attitude as foundational to success.

Personal Observances:

_____
_____
_____

April 28

Truth

Inspiration:	**2 John 1:3** - Grace, mercy and peace from God the Father and from Jesus Christ, the Father's Son, will be with us in **truth** and love.
National Day:	National Braveheart's Day
Anniversary:	1930 – First organized night baseball game is played in Kansas
Born Today:	1758 – President James Monroe (5)
Motivation:	"The truth may hurt for a little while, but a lie hurts forever." – Unknown
Battle's Bullet:	Don't let the "pressure to please" overcome your common sense to tell the truth!

Personal Observances:

_____
_____
_____

April 29

Victorious

Inspiration: **Revelation 2:7** - Whoever has ears, let them hear what the Spirit says to the churches. To the one who is **victorious**, I will give the right to eat from the tree of life, which is in the paradise of God.

National Day: National Zipper Day

Anniversary: 1953 – First experimental television broadcast in 3-D

Born Today: 1951 – Dale Earnhardt - racing

Motivation: "If you're going through hell, keep going." – Winston Churchill

Battle's Bullet: There is synergy in teamwork. 2+2 can be greater than 4.

Personal Observances:
_____
_____
_____

April  30

Thankful

Inspiration:	**Colossians 4:2** - Devote yourselves to prayer, being watchful and **thankful**.
National Day:	National Honesty Day
Anniversary:	1975 – U.S. evacuates Saigon ending presence in Vietnam war
Born Today:	1916 – Robert Shaw - conductor
Motivation:	"A happy heart is a thankful heart, and a thankful heart is a happy heart." – Kent Greene
Battle's Bullet:	**Returning the Favor** acknowledges gifts we have received from others unknown and known, whereas paying it forward can overlook those gifts.

Personal Observances:

_____
_____
_____

MAY

May 1

Joy

Inspiration: **Psalm 28:7** - The Lord is my strength and my shield; my heart trusts in him, and he helps me. My heart leaps for **joy**, and with my song I praise him.

National Day: May Day

Anniversary: 1939 – First appearance of Batman in Detective Comics #27

Born Today: 1852 – Calamity Jane (Martha Jane Canary) - sharpshooter

Motivation: "Joy is a decision, a really brave one, about how you're going to respond to life." – Wess Stafford

Battle's Bullet: Life has its ups and downs, risks and rewards, joy and suffering--and no one will change that.

Personal Observances:

_____
_____
_____

May 2

Honor

Inspiration:	**Proverbs 13:18** - Whoever disregards discipline comes to poverty and shame, but whoever heeds correction is **honor**ed.
National Day:	National Life Insurance Day
Anniversary:	1887 – Celluloid film used in Edison's Kinetoscope is patented by Hannibal Goodwin
Born Today:	1844 – Elijah McCoy - inventor
Motivation:	"Honor bespeaks worth. Confidence begets truth. Service brings satisfaction. Cooperation proves the quality of leadership." – James Cash (JC) Penney
Battle's Bullet:	When you are giving your best effort in serving others and working to improve yourself, you will stand out like a beacon from a lighthouse on a very dark night.

Personal Observances:

_____

_____

_____

May  3

Heart

Inspiration: **Proverbs 15:14** - The discerning **heart** seeks knowledge, but the mouth of a fool feeds on folly.

National Day: National Paranormal Day

Anniversary: 1845 – Macon B. Allen is the first African-American admitted as a lawyer in Massachusetts

Born Today: 1903 – Bing Crosby - entertainer

Motivation: "Sometimes God doesn't change your situation because He is trying to change your heart." – Unknown

Battle's Bullet: We never know which of our brothers and sisters are suffering from a disease or another issue, which makes our interaction with others more important than we might otherwise believe.

Personal Observances:
___
___
___

May 4

Hope

Inspiration: 1 Timothy 4:10 - That is why we labor and strive, because we have put our **hope** in the living God, who is the Savior of all people, and especially of those who believe.

National Day: National Star Wars Day

Anniversary: 1869 – Cincinnati Red Stockings win their first professional game 45-9 over the Great Western Ball Club

Born Today: 1796 – Horace Mann – public school pioneer

Motivation: "Earth's troubles fade in the light of Heaven's hope." -Billy Graham

Battle's Bullet: I hope you will discover the opportunity of influencing the future far earlier than I did.

Personal Observances:
___
___
___

May 5

Courage

Inspiration: **Philippians 1:20** - I eagerly expect and hope that I will in no way be ashamed, but will have sufficient **courage** so that now as always Christ will be exalted in my body, whether by life or by death.

National Day: National Astronauts Day

Anniversary: 1891 – Carnegie Hall opens in New York City

Born Today: 1865 – Nellie Bly – author and adventurer

Motivation: "Fear is a reaction. Courage is a decision." – Winston Churchill

Battle's Bullet: Sometimes, life deals us a second chance or a mulligan, and hopefully, we hit a better second shot.

Personal Observances:
___
___
___

May 6

Act

Inspiration: **James 2:22** - You see that his faith and his **act**ions were working together, and his faith was made complete by what he did.

National Day: National Nurses Day

Anniversary: 1837 – First steel plow is created by blacksmith, John Deere

Born Today: 1915 – Orson Welles – actor and director

Motivation: "It is the greatest of all mistakes to do nothing when you can only do a little. Do what you can!" – Sydney Smith

Battle's Bullet: Those who don't do their best all of the time hurt themselves and will pay a hefty price for it.

Personal Observances:
_____
_____
_____

May 7

Fearless

Inspiration: **Jeremiah 39:17** - But I will rescue you on that day, declares the Lord; you will **not** be given into the hands of those you **fear**.

National Day: National Paste-Up Day

Anniversary: 1700 – William Penn advocates for the emancipation of blacks

Born Today: 1909 – Edwin Land – inventor and scientist

Motivation: "Understand that not everything is meant to be understood. Live, let go, and don't worry about what you can't change." – livelifehappy.com

Battle's Bullet: Too often, we fear a dream *withheld* to us, for one reason or another, will be *denied* to us for a lifetime. It does not have to be that way.

Personal Observances:
_____
_____
_____

May 8

Humble

Inspiration: Matthew 23:12 - For those who exalt themselves will be **humble**d, and those who **humble** themselves will be exalted.

National Day: National Student Nurse Day

Anniversary: 1945 – VE Day as Germany surrenders to the Allies

Born Today: 1884 – President Harry Truman (31)

Motivation: "Blessed are they who see beautiful things in humble places where other people see nothing." – Camille Pissarro

Battle's Bullet: The more often we realize that our actions are examples and contemplate their effect, the better we will perform and the more positive impact we will have on others.

Personal Observances:
___
___
___

May 9

Faith - Faithful

Inspiration:	**Hebrews 11: 1-3** - Now **faith** is confidence in what we hope for and assurance about what we do not see. This is what the ancients were commended for. By **faith** we understand that the universe was formed at God's command, so that what is seen was not made out of what was visible...
National Day:	National Lost Sock Memorial Day
Anniversary:	1914 - Mother's Day is established by the U. S. Congress and proclaimed by President Woodrow Wilson
Born Today:	1800 – John Brown - abolitionist
Motivation:	"Don't let your faith dim in the storm of life." – Bruce D. Porter
Battle's Bullet:	I don't know how people without faith survive the adversities in life!

Personal Observances:
___
___
___

May 10

Provision

Inspiration:	1 Peter 4:11 - If anyone speaks, they should do so as one who speaks the very words of God. If anyone serves, they should do so with the strength God **provide**s, so that in all things God may be praised through Jesus Christ. To him be the glory and the power for ever and ever. Amen.
National Day:	National Clean Up Your Room Day
Anniversary:	1869 – Transcontinental railroad is completed with the "golden spike" in Utah
Born Today:	1958 – Ellen Ochoa - astronaut
Motivation:	"The provision is in the promises." – Derek Prince
Battle's Bullet:	If we don't manage our time, our time will manage us.

Personal Observances:

_____
_____
_____

May  11

Mercy

Inspiration: Matthew 5:7 - Blessed are the merciful, for they will be shown **mercy**.

National Day: National Eat What You Want Day

Anniversary: 1929 – Regular television broadcasts three nights a week begin

Born Today: 1861 – Frederick Russell Burnham - adventurer

Motivation: "Mercy and forgiveness must be free and unmerited to the wrongdoer. If the wrongdoer has to do something to merit it, then it isn't mercy." - Timothy Keller

Battle's Bullet: The more trials that I have experienced, and the more I see our Lord's hand carrying me through them, the more motivated I am to grow closer to Him.

Personal Observances:
_____
_____
_____

May 12

Forgiveness

Inspiration: **Colossians 3:13** - Bear with each other and **forgive** one another if any of you has a grievance against someone. **Forgive** as the Lord forgave you.

National Day: National Limerick Day

Anniversary: 1777 – Ice cream is first advertised in the *New York Gazette*

Born Today: 1820 – Florence Nightingale – founder of modern nursing

Motivation: "Forgive others not because they deserve forgiveness; but because you deserve peace." – Jonathan Lochwood Huie

Battle's Bullet: Winning in the short term by avoiding personal responsibility leads to a false sense of success.

Personal Observances:
_____
_____
_____

May 13

Grace

Inspiration: 1 Peter 5:10 - And the God of all **grace**, who called you to his eternal glory in Christ, after you have suffered a little while, will himself restore you and make you strong, firm and steadfast.

National Day: National Apple Pie Day

Anniversary: 1958 – Velcro is trademarked

Born Today: 1914 – Joe Louis - boxer

Motivation: "God's great Grace is working in your greatest weakness." – Joseph Prince

Battle's Bullet: We have an opportunity to lift people and reflect on the Grace that we receive in our lives.

Personal Observances:
___
___
___

May  14

Love

Inspiration:	**John 3:16** -For God so **love**d the world that he gave his one and only Son, that whoever believes in him shall not perish but have eternal life.
National Day:	National Dance Like a Chicken Day
Anniversary:	1853 – Gail Borden patents the process for condensed milk
Born Today:	1944 – George Lucas – director, screenwriter and producer
Motivation:	"Spread love everywhere you go. Let no one ever come to you without leaving happier." – Mother Teresa
Battle's Bullet:	I know that God loves me more than I deserve and that He is with me for my benefit all of the time.

Personal Observances:

_____
_____
_____

May  15

Rejoice

Inspiration: **Proverbs 29:2** - When the righteous thrive, the people **rejoice**; when the wicked rule, the people groan.

National Day: Peace Officers Memorial Day

Anniversary: 1905 – Las Vegas is founded

Born Today: 1856 – L. Frank Baum – author – *The Wizard of Oz*

Motivation: "You can complain because roses have thorns, or you can rejoice because thorns have roses." – Tom Wilson

Battle's Bullet: I am mindful that as I go through my walk filled with joy and trials, other people observe my actions. I wish I had realized it much earlier in my life.

Personal Observances:
___
___
___

May 16

Adversity – Trials - Obstacles

Inspiration: Isaiah 30:20 - Although the Lord gives you the bread of **adversity** and the water of affliction, your teachers will be hidden no more; with your own eyes you will see them.

National Day: National Barbecue Day

Anniversary: 1929 – First Academy Awards ceremony is held in Hollywood

Born Today: 1905 – Henry Fonda - actor

Motivation: "As with the butterfly, adversity is necessary to build character in people." – Joseph B. Wirthlin

Battle's Bullet: What will our attitude be when things don't go our way and adversity smacks us right in the face? That is a real test of our character.

Personal Observances:
_____
_____
_____

May  17

Encouragement

Inspiration: **Colossians 2:2** - My goal is that they may be **encourage**d in heart and united in love, so that they may have the full riches of complete understanding, in order that they may know the mystery of God, namely, Christ

National Day: National Pack Rat Day

Anniversary: 1875 – First Kentucky Derby race is run

Born Today: 1903 – Cool Papa Bell - baseball

Motivation: "It is not the mountain we conquer, but ourselves." - Edmund Hillary

Battle's Bullet: We need to surround ourselves with people who will encourage us and avoid those who add fear, uncertainty, and doubt into our thinking.

Personal Observances:
___
___
___

May 18

Endurance

Inspiration:	**2 Corinthians 1:6** - If we are distressed, it is for your comfort and salvation; if we are comforted, it is for your comfort, which produces in you patient **endurance** of the same sufferings we suffer.
National Day:	National Visit Your Relatives Day
Anniversary:	1980 – Mt. St. Helens erupts killing 57 people
Born Today:	1897 – Frank Capra – film director
Motivation:	"Endurance is nobler than strength, and patience than beauty." – John Ruskin
Battle's Bullet:	We have to face, endure, overcome, and learn from our trials and challenges to build better lives in the future.

Personal Observances:

_____
_____
_____

May 19

Example

Inspiration:	**1 Timothy 4:12** - Don't let anyone look down on you because you are young, but set an **example** for the believers in speech, in conduct, in love, in faith and in purity.
National Day:	National Devil's Food Cake Day
Anniversary:	1921 – U.S. Congress restricts immigration and establishes a quota system
Born Today:	1795 – Johns Hopkins - philanthropist
Motivation:	"The world is changed by your example, not your opinion." – Paulo Coelho
Battle's Bullet:	We never know when someone is looking to us as an example, which means that we should always act as if that moment is it.

Personal Observances:

_____
_____
_____

May 20

Grow

Inspiration: **1 Peter 2:2** -Like newborn babies, crave pure spiritual milk, so that by it you may **grow** up in your salvation,

National Day: National Be a Millionaire Day

Anniversary: 1873 – The first pair of blue jeans is patented by Levi Strauss and Jacob Davis

Born Today: 1908 – Jimmy Stewart – actor and military

Motivation: "If you want something you've never had, you've got to do something you've never done." – President Thomas Jefferson

Battle's Bullet: God brings experiences to us to teach us lessons. The question is, how many times do we need a trial to learn one lesson?

Personal Observances:
_____
_____
_____

May 21

Overcomer

Inspiration:	**Jeremiah 15:20** - I will make you a wall to this people, a fortified wall of bronze; they will fight against you but will not **overcome** you, for I am with you to rescue and save you," declares the Lord.
National Day:	National Red Cross Founders Day
Anniversary:	1927 – Charles Lindbergh lands in Paris becoming the first person to fly solo across the Atlantic Ocean
Born Today:	1916 – Harold Robbins - author
Motivation:	"Overcoming obstacles starts with a positive attitude and faith that God will see you through." – picturequotes.com
Battle's Bullet:	We can't control our surrounding environment as we traverse the path to our success, but we can control how we respond, adapt, and overcome all challenges!

Personal Observances:

_____
_____
_____

May  22

Patience

Inspiration:	Psalm 40:1 - **For the director of music. Of David. A psalm.** I waited **patient**ly for the LORD; he turned to me and heard my cry.
National Day:	National Solitaire Day
Anniversary:	1843 – First wagon train leaves Independence, Missouri bound for Oregon
Born Today:	1928 – T. Boone Pickens – business and philanthropy
Motivation:	"When you're tempted to lose patience with someone, think how patient God has been with you all of the time." – Unknown
Battle's Bullet:	Maturity gives us the luxury of being more patient in a situation, enabling us to respond better to it.

Personal Observances:

_____
_____
_____

May  23

Peace

Inspiration: **Philippians 4:7** - And the **peace** of God, which transcends all understanding, will guard your hearts and your minds in Christ Jesus.

National Day: National Lucky Penny Day

Anniversary: 1785 – Benjamin Franklin invents bi-focal glasses

Born Today: 1908 – John Bardeen – inventor of transistor

Motivation: "Peace is the result of retraining your mind to process life as it is, rather than as you think it should be." – Wayne W. Dyer

Battle's Bullet: There is nothing on this earth that will provide rest and peace in the darkest hour.

Personal Observances:
_____
_____
_____

May 24

Stand Firm

Inspiration:	Matthew 24:13 - but the one who **stands firm** to the end will be saved.
National Day:	Brothers' Day
Anniversary:	1844 – Samuel Morse sends the first telegraph message of "What hath God wrought?"
Born Today:	1878 – Lillian Gilbreath – psychologist and engineer
Motivation:	"Beloved, God has never failed to act but in goodness and love. When all means fail, His love prevails. Hold fast to your faith. Stand fast in His word. There is no other hope in this world." – Dave Wilkerson
Battle's Bullet:	Encourage people to show up, stand up, and speak up to defend our gift of freedom against all who seek to destroy it for ideals that have never worked anywhere in the world.

Personal Observances:

_____
_____
_____

May 25

Wisdom

Inspiration: **Proverbs 2:12 - Wisdom** will save you from the ways of wicked men, from men whose words are perverse,

National Day: National Missing Children's Day

Anniversary: 1961 – President John Kennedy declares the goal to land an American on the moon by the end of the decade

Born Today: 1803 – Ralph Waldo Emerson - author

Motivation: "To acquire knowledge, one must study; but to acquire wisdom, one must observe." – Marilyn Vos Savant

Battle's Bullet: If common sense was common, we wouldn't talk about it.

Personal Observances:
_____
_____
_____

May 26

Perseverance

Inspiration: **James 1:2-8** - Consider it pure joy, my brothers and sisters, whenever you face trials of many kinds, because you know that the testing of your faith produces **perseverance**. Let perseverance finish its work so that you may be mature and complete, not lacking anything. ...

National Day: National Paper Airplane Day
MEMORIAL Day (last Monday)

Anniversary: 1940 – Igor Sikorsky designed helicopter, first flies successfully in the United States

Born Today: 1907 – John Wayne - actor

1951 – Sally Ride - astronaut

Motivation: "If plan A fails, remember there are 25 more letters." – Unknown

Battle's Bullet: Persist always in the face of adversity.

Personal Observances:
_____
_____
_____

May 27

Trustworthy - Trust

Inspiration: **Psalm 62:8** - **Trust** in him at all times, you people; pour out your hearts to him, for God is our refuge.

National Day: National Cellophane Tape Day

Anniversary: 1937 – The Golden Gate bridge is opened in San Francisco

Born Today: 1923 – Henry Kissinger - statesman

Motivation: "Trust is the glue of life. It is the most essential ingredient in effective communication. It's the foundational principle in all relationships." – Stephen Covey

Battle's Bullet: Only by accepting responsibility for our actions and seeing the resulting increase in trust in us, and the resulting benefits will confirm it is the appropriate action in every circumstance.

Personal Observances:
___
___
___

May 28

Truth

Inspiration:	**Psalm 145:18** - The Lord is near to all who call on him, to all who call on him in **truth**.
National Day:	National Hamburger Day
Anniversary:	1892 – John Muir and others found Sierra Club to conserve nature
Born Today:	1888 – Jim Thorpe - athlete
Motivation:	"Truth is so obscured nowadays and lies so well established that unless we love the truth we shall never recognize it." – Blaise Pascal
Battle's Bullet:	The thing that makes uncovering a half-truth difficult is professional liars' ability to tell their stories with a straight face.

Personal Observances:

_____
_____
_____

May 29

Victorious

Inspiration: **Revelation 2:17** - Whoever has ears, let them hear what the Spirit says to the churches. To the one who is **victorious**, I will give some of the hidden manna. I will also give that person a white stone with a new name written on it, known only to the one who receives it.

National Day: National Paperclip Day

Anniversary: 1790 – U. S. Constitution is ratified by Rhode Island, the last of the 13 original colonies

Born Today: 1917 – President John F. Kennedy (35)
1736 – Patrick Henry – "Give me liberty, or give me death!"
1903 – Bob Hope - entertainer

Motivation: "Accept challenges so you can feel the exhilaration of victory." – George S. Patton

Battle's Bullet: A good attitude is the starting point of every success.

Personal Observances:
_____
_____
_____

May 30

Thankful

Inspiration:	**2 Corinthians 4:15** - All this is for your benefit, so that the grace that is reaching more and more people may cause **thanksgiving** to overflow to the glory of God.
National Day:	National Creativity Day
Anniversary:	1922 – Lincoln Memorial is dedicated in Washington, D.C. by U.S. Chief Justice Taft
Born Today:	1908 – Mel Blanc - entertainer
Motivation:	"Gratitude is the healthiest of all human emotions. The more you express gratitude for what you have, the more likely you will have even more to express gratitude for." – Zig Ziglar
Battle's Bullet:	I'm thankful my formal education occurred before today's partisan brawls to influence curriculum based on politics and vast sums of money.

Personal Observances:

_____
_____
_____

May 31

Good Cheer

Inspiration: **Proverbs 17:22** - A **cheer**ful heart is good medicine, but a crushed spirit dries up the bones.

National Day: National Smile Day

Anniversary: 1879 – Madison Square Garden dedicated to President Madison opens in New York

Born Today: 1930 – Clint Eastwood – actor and director

Motivation: "The man who radiates good cheer, who makes life happier wherever he meets it, is always a man of vision and faith." – Ella Wheeler Wilcox

Battle's Bullet: SMILE. Always say please and thank you, and we'll find more doors opened to us.

Personal Observances:
_____
_____
_____

JUNE

June 1

Joy

Inspiration: **Psalm 94:19** - When anxiety was great within me, your consolation brought me **joy**.

National Day: National Go Barefoot Day

Anniversary: 1869 – Thomas Edison patents first vote recorder

Born Today: 1801 – Brigham Young

Motivation: "Joy comes when we choose to live in harmony with God's eternal plan." – Russell M. Nelson

Battle's Bullet: We can be as enthusiastic as we want, but if we don't positively believe we can accomplish something; we will fall short in the effort.

Personal Observances:
___
___
___

June 2

Honor

Inspiration:	Matthew 15:4 - For God said, '**Honor** your father and mother' and 'Anyone who curses their father or mother is to be put to death.'
National Day:	National Bubba Day
Anniversary:	1857 – Chain stitch single thread sewing machine is patented by James Gibbs
Born Today:	1904 – Johnny Weissmuller – athlete, actor (Tarzan)
Motivation:	"It is not the honor you take with you, but the heritage you leave behind." – Branch Rickey
Battle's Bullet:	If we want to receive loyalty, we must first be loyal to others.

Personal Observances:
_____
_____
_____

June 3

Heart

Inspiration: Ecclesiastes 10:2 - The **heart** of the wise inclines to the right, but the **heart** of the fool to the left.

National Day: National Repeat Day

Anniversary: 1888 – *Casey at the Bat* is first published in the *San Francisco Examiner*

Born Today: 1936 – Larry McMurtry - author

Motivation: "Being humble is much more than being wise! Because God doesn't need a proud mouth that speaks much. But a kind heart that LISTENS." – Unknown

Battle's Bullet: The path toward excellence has challenges, demands, and uncertainty. It is not for the timid or faint-hearted, but for those who are willing to extend themselves and produce excellence consistently.

Personal Observances:
_____
_____
_____

June 4

Hope

Inspiration: **Jeremiah 29:11** - For I know the plans I have for you," declares the Lord, "plans to prosper you and not to harm you, plans to give you **hope** and a future.

National Day: National Hug Your Cat Day

Anniversary: 1896 – Henry Ford drives his first car in Detroit

Born Today: 1945 – Anthony Braxton – musician and composer

Motivation: "Thanks be to God, there is hope today; this very hour you can choose Him and serve Him." – Dwight L. Moody

Battle's Bullet: The hope of life being fair is attractive but unattainable regardless of who promises it.

Personal Observances:
_____
_____
_____

June 5

Courage

Inspiration:	**Joshua 10:25** - Joshua said to them, "Do not be afraid; do not be discouraged. Be strong and **courage**ous. This is what the Lord will do to all the enemies you are going to fight."
National Day:	National Gingerbread Day
Anniversary:	1968 – Presidential candidate Robert F. Kennedy is shot and dies the next day
Born Today:	1850 – Pat Garrett - lawman
Motivation:	"Courage is doing what you are afraid to do. There can be no courage unless you are afraid." – Eddie Rickenbacker
Battle's Bullet:	Everything we do today impacts our future.

Personal Observances:
___
___
___

June 6

Act

Inspiration: **Psalm 71:18** -Even when I am old and gray, do not forsake me, my God, till I declare your power to the next generation, your mighty **act**s to all who are to come.

National Day: D-Day & Higher Education Day

Anniversary: 1944 – D-Day invasion of France

Born Today: 1755 – Nathan Hale – "My only regret is I have but one life to give for my country."

Motivation: "Fortune favors the bold." – Roman Poet Virgil

Battle's Bullet: I did is better than I will.

Personal Observances:

_____
_____
_____

JUNE 7

Fearless

Inspiration: **Proverbs 3:7** - Do **not** be wise in your own eyes; **fear** the Lord and shun evil.

National Day: National Chocolate Ice Cream Day

Anniversary: 1942 – Battle of Midway ends in U.S. victory establishing dominance of air power

Born Today: 1900 – Frederick Terman - engineer

Motivation: "A man really believes not what he recites in his creed, but only the things he is ready to die for." – Richard Wurmbrand

Battle's Bullet: Nobody said life wouldn't be semi-tough – a corollary to Billy Clyde Puckett in *Semi-Tough*.

Personal Observances:
___
___
___

June 8

Humble

Inspiration:	1 Peter 5:5-6 - In the same way, you who are younger, submit yourselves to your elders. All of you, clothe yourselves with humility toward one another, because, "God opposes the proud but shows favor to the **humble**." **Humble** yourselves, therefore, under God's mighty hand, that he may lift you up in due time.
National Day:	National Best Friends Day
Anniversary:	1789 – A proposed Bill of Rights is introduced to Congress by James Madison
Born Today:	1867 – Frank Lloyd Wright - architect
Motivation:	"Humble yourself or life will do it for you." – Unknown
Battle's Bullet:	Why say boo boo when boo will do?

Personal Observances:

_____
_____
_____

June 9

Faith - Faithful

Inspiration: 1 Samuel 12:24 - But be sure to fear the Lord and serve him **faith**fully with all your heart; consider what great things he has done for you.

National Day: National Donald Duck Day

Anniversary: 1869 – First root beer is sold by Charles Hires in Philadelphia

Born Today: 1916 – Robert McNamara - statesman

Motivation: "Faith is building on what you know is here so you can reach what you know is there." – Cullen Hightower

Battle's Bullet: My reliable personal experience and evidence of my savior Jesus Christ, the Holy Spirit, the Scriptures, and examples of fellow believers cement my faith for provision to withstand any trial.

Personal Observances:
___
___
___

June 10

Provision

Inspiration: **Genesis 22:14** - So Abraham called that place The Lord Will Provide. And to this day it is said, "On the mountain of the Lord it will be **provided**."

National Day: National Iced Tea Day

Anniversary: 1752 – Benjamin Franklin tests his kite with a lightning conductor

Born Today: 1895 – Hattie McDaniel - actress

Motivation: "God has promised to provide all our needs. What we don't have now we don't need now." – Elisabeth Elliot

Battle's Bullet: A positive outlook on life provides the confidence to maximize the opportunities presented to us and the inner strength to face life's difficulties.

Personal Observances:
_____
_____
_____

June 11

Mercy

Inspiration: **Psalm 51:1** - Have **mercy** on me, O God, according to your unfailing love; according to your great compassion blot out my transgressions.

National Day: National Making Life Beautiful Day

Anniversary: 1742 – Benjamin Franklin invents the Franklin stove

Born Today: 1913 – Vince Lombardi - coach

Motivation: "Sometimes due to God's mercy, the time in God's plan can be stretched or extended." - Sunday Adelaja

Battle's Bullet: We should help all who we can, where we can, and how we can.

Personal Observances:
___
___
___

June  12

Forgiveness

Inspiration:	Luke 23:34 - Jesus said, "Father, **forgive** them, for they do not know what they are doing." And they divided up his clothes by casting lots.
National Day:	National Loving Day
Anniversary:	1859 – The Comstock Silver Lode is the first major silver strike in the U.S
Born Today:	1924 – President George H. W. Bush (41)
Motivation:	"Holding a grudge doesn't make you strong; it makes you bitter. Forgiveness doesn't make you weak; it sets you free." – Dave Willis
Battle's Bullet:	None of us can be the perfect example like Christ, but we can all strive to be the best example we can for others' benefit.

Personal Observances:

_____
_____
_____

JUNE 13

Grace

Inspiration:	**Romans 5:15** - But the gift is not like the trespass. For if the many died by the trespass of the one man, how much more did God's **grace** and the gift that came by the **grace** of the one man, Jesus Christ, overflow to the many!
National Day:	National Arc of Lights Day
Anniversary:	1967 – Thurgood Marshall is the first African-American nominated to the Supreme Court.
Born Today:	1786 – Winfield Scott - General
Motivation:	"Grace doesn't seem fair until you need some." – Bob Goff
Battle's Bullet:	Our impact on others with our gifts is our gift back to God.

Personal Observances:

_____
_____
_____

June  14

Love

Inspiration:	Mark 12:30 - **Love** the Lord your God with all your heart and with all your soul and with all your mind and with all your strength.
National Day:	Flag Day & Army Birthday
Anniversary:	1777 – Stars and Stripes designed by Francis Hopkinson is adopted by the Continental Congress
Born Today:	1946 – President Donald Trump (45)
Motivation:	"Love is fathomless; a unique emotion evoking unparalleled happiness." – Jen Ross
Battle's Bullet:	Love and care for your mother and father. They unconditionally love you and deserve your love, respect, and attention.

Personal Observances:

_____
_____
_____

June  15

Rejoice

Inspiration:	**John 16:20** - Very truly I tell you, you will weep and mourn while the world **rejoice**s. You will grieve, but your grief will turn to joy.
National Day:	National Photography Day
Anniversary:	1844 – Vulcanization of rubber is patented by Charles Goodyear.
Born Today:	1923 – Erroll Garner – jazz pianist
Motivation:	"Thou wilt always rejoice in the evening if thou has spent the day profitably." – Thomas a Kempis
Battle's Bullet:	Maturity has taught me I can trust Him to take care of me every day better than I deserve.

Personal Observances:
___
___
___

June 16

Adversity – Trials - Obstacles

Inspiration: 2 Peter 2:9 - if this is so, then the Lord knows how to rescue the godly from **trial**s and to hold the unrighteous for punishment on the day of judgment.

National Day: National Fudge Day

Anniversary: 1858 – Abraham Lincoln's nomination speech includes line, "a house divided against itself cannot stand."

Born Today: 1738 – Mary Katharine Goddard – printer and publisher

Motivation: "Sometimes adversity is what you need to face in order to become successful." – Zig Ziglar

Battle's Bullet: Every episode of adversity I have experienced, while painful at the moment, has positively affected my life.

Personal Observances:
_____
_____
_____

June 17

Encouragement

Inspiration: **2 Corinthians 13:11** - Finally, brothers and sisters, rejoice! Strive for full restoration, **encourage** one another, be of one mind, live in peace. And the God of love and peace will be with you.

National Day: National Garbage Man Day

Anniversary: 1579 – Francis Drake lands in northern California

Born Today: 1943 – Newt Gingrich – politician, author, teacher

Motivation: "Be awesome today. You might inspire someone else and not even know it." – Susie Glennan

Battle's Bullet: Encouraging others to pursue their dreams is one of the greatest gifts we can bestow upon them.

Personal Observances:
___
___
___

June 18

Endurance

Inspiration: **2 Timothy 3:10** - You, however, know all about my teaching, my way of life, my purpose, faith, patience, love, **endurance**,

National Day: National Go Fishing Day

Anniversary: 1928 – Amelia Earhart is the first woman to fly solo across the Atlantic Ocean

Born Today: 1924 – George Mikan - basketball

Motivation: "Without patient endurance, even the smallest thing becomes unbearable. A lot depends on attitude." – Dalai Lama

Battle's Bullet: My life experiences helped me to endure more than I ever believed I could.

Personal Observances:
_____
_____
_____

JUNE 19

Example

Inspiration: Philippians 3:17 - Join together in following my **example**, brothers and sisters, and just as you have us as a model, keep your eyes on those who live as we do.

National Day: Juneteenth

Anniversary: 1865 – Union general Gordon Granger lands in Galveston, Texas and pronounces the slaves free. Juneteenth is the holiday celebrating the end of slavery in the U.S.

Born Today: 1903 – Lou Gehrig - baseball

Motivation: "Leadership means setting an example. When you find yourself in a position of leadership people will follow your every move." – Lee Iacocca

Battle's Bullet: Are the people observing us seeing the example we want them to view?

Personal Observances:
_____
_____
_____

June 20

Grow

Inspiration:	2 Thessalonians 1:3 - We ought always to thank God for you, brothers and sisters, and rightly so, because your faith is **grow**ing more and more, and the love all of you have for one another is increasing.
National Day:	American Eagle Day
Anniversary:	1782 – Eagle and Great Seal of the U.S. are selected and approved by Congress
Born Today:	1925 – Audie Murphy – war hero and actor
Motivation:	"The only person you should ever compare yourself to is the person you used to be." – Unknown
Battle's Bullet:	True leaders are concerned about growing their people.

Personal Observances:

_____
_____
_____

June 21

Overcomer

Inspiration: John 1:5 - The light shines in the darkness, and the darkness has not **overcome** it.

National Day: National Daylight Appreciation Day

Anniversary: 1788 – U. S. Constitution takes effect with the ratification by New Hampshire

Born Today: 1859 – Henry Tanner - painter

Motivation: "In the depth of winter, I finally learned that within me lay an invincible summer." – Albert Camus

Battle's Bullet: If we grow normally, we will better address more considerable challenges because we learn how to overcome them with His help.

Personal Observances:
_____
_____
_____

June 22

Patience

Inspiration:	**Proverbs 25:15** - Through **patience** a ruler can be persuaded, and a gentle tongue can break a bone.
National Day:	National HVAC Tech Day
Anniversary:	1944 – President Roosevelt signs the "GI Bill of Rights"
Born Today:	1906 – Anne Morrow Lindbergh – author and aviator
Motivation:	"Patience is not the ability to wait, but the ability to keep a good attitude while waiting." – Unknown
Battle's Bullet:	Learn the difference between patiently persisting in your actions and overexerting your ambitions. The first leads to long-term success and healthy relationships. The second only rewards you materially in the short term.

Personal Observances:

_____
_____
_____

June 23

Peace

Inspiration:	**Romans 15:13** - May the God of hope fill you with all joy and **peace** as you trust in him, so that you may overflow with hope by the power of the Holy Spirit.
National Day:	National Hydration Day
Anniversary:	1868 – Christopher Sholes patents the first successful typewriter
Born Today:	1940 – Wilma Rudolph – Olympic athlete
Motivation:	"A Christian brings peace to others. Not only peace, but also, love, kindness, faithfulness and joy." – Pope Francis
Battle's Bullet:	Life is full of mysteries. There are things seen that drive us crazy and things unseen that gives us a peace we can entrust for our eternity.

Personal Observances:

_____
_____
_____

June  24

Stand Firm

Inspiration:	**Galatians 5:1** - It is for freedom that Christ has set us free. **Stand firm**, then, and do not let yourselves be burdened again by a yoke of slavery.
National Day:	National Pralines Day
Anniversary:	1853 – President Franklin Pierce completes the Gadsden purchase acquiring land from Mexico in current Arizona and New Mexico
Born Today:	1897 – Daniel Ludwig - shipping
Motivation:	"You cannot run away from weakness; you must some time fight it out or perish; and if that be so, why not now, and where you stand?" – Robert Louis Stevenson
Battle's Bullet:	Too often, we think if we stand and watch, God will take care of us. He wants us to move forward with faith in Him.

Personal Observances:

_____
_____
_____

June 25

Wisdom

Inspiration:	**Proverbs 2:6** - For the Lord gives **wisdom**; from his mouth come knowledge and understanding.
National Day:	National Catfish Day
Anniversary:	1876 – Custer's Last Stand at the Little Big Horn
Born Today:	1925 – Robert Venturi - architect
Motivation:	"I discovered I always have choices and sometimes it's only a choice of attitude." – Judith M. Knowlton
Battle's Bullet:	It is frustrating to observe people who don't know or care to learn from the wisdom of the ages. We can't abandon our efforts to help others based on the rejection of a few.

Personal Observances:

_____

_____

_____

June  26

Perseverance

Inspiration: **James 5:11** - As you know, we count as blessed those who have persevered. You have heard of Job's **perseverance** and have seen what the Lord finally brought about. The Lord is full of compassion and mercy.

National Day: National Beautician's Day

Anniversary: 1933 – President Roosevelt signs the Federal Credit Union Act, which created credit unions

Born Today: 1911 – Babe Didrikson Zaharias- golf

Motivation: "Victory belongs to the most persevering." – Napoleon Bonaparte

Battle's Bullet: The Only difference in can and can't is our **T**emperament.

Personal Observances:
___
___
___

JUNE 27

Trustworthy - Trust

Inspiration: **Psalm 25:1-2** - In you, Lord my God, I put my **trust**. I **trust** in you; do not let me be put to shame, nor let my enemies' triumph over me.

National Day: National Sunglasses Day

Anniversary: 1972 – Early electronic video game, Atari, is created by Nolan Bushnell and Ted Dabney

Born Today: 1880 – Helen Keller – author and educator

Motivation: "The most expensive thing in the world is trust. It can take years to build and just a matter of seconds to lose." – Unknown

Battle's Bullet: Recognize no earthly institution is worthy of total trust.

Personal Observances:
_____
_____
_____

June  28

Truth

Inspiration:	**2 Timothy 2:15** - Do your best to present yourself to God as one approved, a worker who does not need to be ashamed and who correctly handles the word of **truth**.
National Day:	National Paul Bunyan Day
Anniversary:	1965 – President Johnson sends first U.S. ground troops to Vietnam
Born Today:	1971 – Elon Musk - entrepreneur
Motivation:	"A real man will be honest no matter how painful the truth is. A coward hides behind lies and deceit." – Unknown
Battle's Bullet:	If I had recognized the truth my actions were examples earlier in life, I would have modified my behavior and made fewer mistakes that embarrass me to remember today.

Personal Observances:
___
___
___

June 29

Victorious

Inspiration:	Revelation 3:5 - The one who is **victorious** will, like them, be dressed in white. I will never blot out the name of that person from the book of life, but will acknowledge that name before my Father and his angels.
National Day:	National Camera Day
Anniversary:	1936 – George M. Cohan is the first artist to receive the Congressional Gold Medal for raising morale and American pride
Born Today:	1868 – George Hale - astronomer
Motivation:	"Adapt, improvise and overcome." – Gunny Highway on *Heartbreak Ridge*
Battle's Bullet:	We will always achieve more with a positive attitude than a negative one.

Personal Observances:
___
___
___

June 30

Thankful

Inspiration: **2 Corinthians 9:11** - You will be enriched in every way so that you can be generous on every occasion, and through us your generosity will result in **thanksgiving** to God.

National Day: Social Media Day

Anniversary: 1936 – *Gone With the Wind* is published by author Margaret Mitchell

Born Today: 1930 – Thomas Sowell – economist and educator

Motivation: "When I started counting my blessings, my whole life turned around." – Willie Nelson

Battle's Bullet: Be VERY grateful for what you have. It doesn't take long to find someone worse off than you are.

Personal Observances:
___
___
___

JULY

July 1

Joy

Inspiration: Psalm 19:8 - The precepts of the Lord are right, giving **joy** to the heart. The commands of the Lord are radiant, giving light to the eyes.

National Day: National Postal Worker Day

Anniversary: 1863 – First day of Battle of Gettysburg

Born Today: 1906 – Estee' Lauder - business

Motivation: "The joy which comes from forgetting ourselves is the best proof of love." – St. Josemaria Escriva

Battle's Bullet: Too often, we eagerly desire a future stage of life and forget to enjoy and appreciate where we are at the moment.

Personal Observances:
_____
_____
_____

July 2

Honor

Inspiration:	**Romans 12:10** - Be devoted to one another in love. **Honor** one another above yourselves.
National Day:	National Anisette Day
Anniversary:	1881 – President James Garfield is shot, and dies 79 days later
Born Today:	1908 – Thurgood Marshall – Supreme Court Justice
Motivation:	"No person was ever honored for what he received. Honor has been the reward for what he gave." – President Calvin Coolidge
Battle's Bullet:	We stand on the shoulders of giants, though imperfect, whose gift to us will be in vain if we do not extend it to the next generations.

Personal Observances:

_____
_____
_____

July 3

Heart

Inspiration: Colossians 3:23 - Whatever you do, work at it with all your **heart**, as working for the Lord, not for human masters,

National Day: National Fried Clam Day

Anniversary: 1863 – Battle of Gettysburg ends in Union victory after Pickett's charge fails

Born Today: 1878 – George M. Cohan - entertainer

Motivation: "A joyful heart is like the sunshine of God's love, the hope of eternal happiness." – Mother Teresa

Battle's Bullet: The radiant light of God shining through that dark wall of clouds, provides us Grace and fills our heart with hope in our hour of need.

Personal Observances:

_____
_____
_____

July 4

Hope

Inspiration:	Matthew 12:21 - In his name the nations will put their **hope**."
National Day:	Independence Day
Anniversary:	1776 – United States Declaration of Independence from Great Britain
Born Today:	1872 – President Calvin Coolidge (30)
Motivation:	"Hope means expectancy when things are otherwise hopeless." – G. K. Chesterton
Battle's Bullet:	I hope that I have given enough breadth, width, and depth of the gifts that I have received to **Return the Favor** to others before completing my course.

Personal Observances:
_____
_____
_____

July 5

Courage

Inspiration: **1 Chronicles 22:13** - Then you will have success if you are careful to observe the decrees and laws that the Lord gave Moses for Israel. Be strong and **courage**ous. Do not be afraid or discouraged.

National Day: National Bikini Day

Anniversary: 1994 – Amazon.com founded by Jeff Bezos

Born Today: 1810 – P. T. Barnum – showman and circus owner

Motivation: "All our dreams can come true if we have the courage to pursue them." – Walt Disney

Battle's Bullet: If you want something tomorrow, invest today to earn it.

Personal Observances:
___
___
___

July  6

Act

Inspiration: Psalm 9:16 - The Lord is known by his **act**s of justice; the wicked are ensnared by the work of their hands.

National Day: National Fried Chicken Day

Anniversary: 1928 – First all-talking movie is shown in New York

Born Today: 1946 – President George W. Bush (43)
1747 – John Paul Jones – U.S. Navy hero in Revolutionary War

Motivation: "One person can make a difference and every person should try." – President John F. Kennedy

Battle's Bullet: It is up to we who have survived our ill-advised actions to temper the next generations' zeal in a way that doesn't repel them from our advice.

Personal Observances:
_____
_____
_____

July 7

Fearless

Inspiration:	**Psalm 34:9** - **Fear** the Lord, you his holy people, for those who **fear** him lack **not**hing.
National Day:	National Father Daughter Take a Walk Day
Anniversary:	1928 – Sliced bread sold for the first time. What was the best thing before it?
Born Today:	1906 – Satchel Paige - Baseball
Motivation:	"If people are doubting how far you will go, go so far that you can't hear them anymore." – Michele Ruiz
Battle's Bullet:	Victims dwell in fear, which paralyzes their ability to progress.

Personal Observances:

_____
_____
_____

July 8

Humble

Inspiration: Isaiah 2:17 - The arrogance of man will be brought low and human pride **humble**d; the Lord alone will be exalted in that day,

National Day: National Chocolate with Almonds Day

Anniversary: 1896 – William Jennings Bryan *Cross of Gold* speech at Democrat National Convention

Born Today: 1839 – John D. Rockefeller - finance

Motivation: "Be strong when you are weak. Be brave when you are scared. Be humble when you are victorious." --Unknown

Battle's Bullet: If we are a good example, we must focus on others more than ourselves because we realize that our actions can either lift people up or bring them down.

Personal Observances:
_____
_____
_____

July 9

Faith - Faithful

Inspiration:	**2 Peter 1:5** - For this very reason, make every effort to add to your **faith** goodness; and to goodness, knowledge
National Day:	National Sugar Cookie Day
Anniversary:	1955 – *Rock Around the Clock* by Bill Haley and the Comets launches rock and roll
Born Today:	1819 – Elias Howe – inventor of the sewing machine
Motivation:	"Faith sees the invisible, believes the unbelievable, and receives the impossible." – Corrie Ten Boom
Battle's Bullet:	He wants us to move with faith in Him that He is in control and provides for our every need according to His plan for us.

Personal Observances:

_____
_____
_____

July 10

Provision

Inspiration: Isaiah 43:2 - When you pass through the waters, I will be with you; and when you pass through the rivers, they will not sweep over you. When you walk through the fire, you will not be burned; the flames will not set you ablaze.

National Day: National Pina Colada Day

Anniversary: 1862 – U.S. began construction of the Central Pacific railroad

Born Today: 1910 – Mary McLeod Bethune - educator

Motivation: "You make the decision with vision and God makes the provision." – Mark Victor Hansen

Battle's Bullet: God loved me before I was even born and continues to provide for me and encourage me that regardless of what happens in this life, He has a place for me with Him in eternity.

Personal Observances:
___
___
___

July 11

Mercy

Inspiration: **Proverbs 28:13** - Whoever conceals their sins does not prosper, but the one who confesses and renounces them finds **mercy**.

National Day: All American Pet Photo Day

Anniversary: 1804 – Vice-President Aaron Burr wounds Alexander Hamilton in a pistol duel. Hamilton dies the next day.

Born Today: 1767 – President John Quincy Adams (6)

Motivation: "The more merciful acts thou dost, the more mercy thou wilt receive." - William Penn

Battle's Bullet: For those who believe in a Creator, we must recognize who we are and the gifts we receive from God.

Personal Observances:
___
___
___

July  12

Forgiveness

Inspiration: 1 John 1:9 - If we confess our sins, he is faithful and just and will **forgive** us our sins and purify us from all unrighteousness.

National Day: National Pecan Pie Day

Anniversary: 1933 – U.S. Congress passes the first minimum wage law of 33 cents per hour

Born Today: 1854 – George Eastman – photographic business
1864 – George Washington Carver - inventor

Motivation: "Forgive others as quickly as you expect God to forgive you." – Unknown

Battle's Bullet: I praise God for every blessing I have received, and I ask for and rely on His grace, as well as his forgiveness for my sins.

Personal Observances:
___
___
___

July 13

Grace

Inspiration: **1 Corinthians 15:10** - But by the **grace** of God I am what I am, and his **grace** to me was not without effect. No, I worked harder than all of them—yet not I, but the **grace** of God that was with me.

National Day: National French Fry Day

Anniversary: 1865 – Horace Greeley advises his readers to "Go west young man"

Born Today: 1935 – Jack Kemp – politics and football

Motivation: "Grace alone brings about every good work in us." – St. Augustine

Battle's Bullet: What we are is God's gift to us. What we become is our gift to God.

Personal Observances:
___
___
___

July  14

Love

Inspiration:	**Psalm 59:16** - But I will sing of your strength, in the morning I will sing of your **love**; for you are my fortress, my refuge in times of trouble.
National Day:	National Tape Measure Day
Anniversary:	1914 – Robert Goddard patents liquid fuel for rockets
Born Today:	1913 – President Gerald Ford (38)
Motivation:	"Love, genuine love doesn't take the shape of a heart, but of a cross." – arkinthedesert.com
Battle's Bullet:	When I focus on others instead of myself, my attitude is better, and my heart is appropriately positioned for service.

Personal Observances:

_____
_____
_____

July 15

Rejoice

Inspiration: **Isaiah 49:13** - Shout for joy, you heavens; **rejoice**, you earth; burst into song, you mountains! For the Lord comforts his people and will have compassion on his afflicted ones.

National Day: National Give Something Away Day

Anniversary: 1912 – Jim Thorpe wins Olympic decathlon after previously winning the pentathlon

Born Today: 1819 – William Thomas Green Morton - surgeon

Motivation: "This is the day that the Lord has made. Let us rejoice and be glad in it." – King David, *Psalm* 118:24

Battle's Bullet: We all have a purpose in life beyond ourselves.

Personal Observances:
___
___
___

July  16

Adversity – Trials - Obstacles

Inspiration: **Romans 14:13** - Therefore let us stop passing judgment on one another. Instead, make up your mind not to put any stumbling block or **obstacle** in the way of a brother or sister.

National Day: National Corn Fritters Day

Anniversary: 1945 – First test of atomic bomb in New Mexico

Born Today: 1907 – Orville Redenbacher – popcorn magnate

Motivation: "Adversity introduces a man to himself." – Albert Einstein

Battle's Bullet: When trouble arises due to our weaknesses, we best serve ourselves when we get closer to Him.

Personal Observances:
___
___
___

July  17

Encouragement

Inspiration: 2 Thessalonians 2:16 - May our Lord Jesus Christ himself and God our Father, who loved us and by his grace gave us eternal **encourage**ment and good hope,

National Day: National Peach Ice Cream Day

Anniversary: 1861 – U.S. Congress authorizes paper money

Born Today: 1763 – John Jacob Astor - business

Motivation: "Encouragement and words of kindness are gifts you can give that can be priceless yet cost nothing." – Unknown

Battle's Bullet: Everyone benefits when they are encouraged.

Personal Observances:
___
___
___

July 18

Endurance

Inspiration: 1 Thessalonians 1:3 - We remember before our God and Father your work produced by faith, your labor prompted by love, and your **endurance** inspired by hope in our Lord Jesus Christ.

National Day: National Sour Candy Day

Anniversary: 1955 – Electric power generated from nuclear energy is first sold

Born Today: 1921 – John Glenn – Astronaut/U.S. Senator

Motivation: "To endure what is unendurable is true endurance." – Proverb

Battle's Bullet: Our lives occur in unequal lengths and realities. We experience ups and downs, swerve to the left and right, submit to discipline and freely have fun, and celebrate joy and endure heartaches as we traverse our individual courses.

Personal Observances:

_____
_____
_____

July 19

Example

Inspiration: **Ephesians 5:1** - Follow God's **example**, therefore, as dearly loved children

National Day: National Ice Cream Day (3rd Sunday)

Anniversary: 1692 – Salem witch trials hang five more people

Born Today: 1814 – Samuel Colt - inventor

Motivation: "The example we set for our kids how to act when things don't go our way is much, much more important than the rules we set for them." - purehappylife.com

Battle's Bullet: Every act is an example to someone.

Personal Observances:

_____
_____
_____

July  20

Grow

Inspiration: **Colossians 1:10** - so that you may live a life worthy of the Lord and please him in every way: bearing fruit in every good work, **grow**ing in the knowledge of God,

National Day: National Moon Day

Anniversary: 1969 – First men land on the moon--Americans on U.S.- launched Apollo 11

Born Today: 1929 – Mike Illitch – entrepreneur and founder of Little Caesar's Pizza

Motivation: "When we are no longer able to change a situation, we are challenged to change ourselves. – Victor E. Frankl

Battle's Bullet: The important thing is to learn what I am supposed to do and grow into the person that God wants me to be before my life is over.

Personal Observances:
___
___
___

July 21

Overcomer

Inspiration: 1 John 2:13 - I am writing to you, fathers, because you know him who is from the beginning. I am writing to you, young men, because you have **overcome** the evil one.

National Day: National Be Someone Day

Anniversary: 1865 – First credited western showdown in Missouri where Wild Bill Hickok shoots Davis Tutt

Born Today: 1899 – Ernest Hemingway - author

Motivation: "If you can find a path with no obstacles, it probably doesn't lead anywhere." – Frank A. Clark

Battle's Bullet: Practice the gift of gratitude after overcoming every adversity.

Personal Observances:
___
___
___

July  22

Patience

Inspiration: 1 Timothy 1:16 - But for that very reason I was shown mercy so that in me, the worst of sinners, Christ Jesus might display his immense **patience** as an example for those who would believe in him and receive eternal life.

National Day: National Hammock Day

Anniversary: 1933 – Wiley Post is the first solo pilot to fly around the world

Born Today: 1923 – Bob Dole – war hero and presidential candidate

Motivation: "Patience is bitter, but its fruit is sweet." – Aristotle

Battle's Bullet: Patience is learned primarily from painful experience.

Personal Observances:
___
___
___

July 23

Peace

Inspiration: **John 14:27** - **Peace** I leave with you; my **peace** I give you. I do not give to you as the world gives. Do not let your hearts be troubled and do not be afraid.

National Day: Gorgeous Grandma Day

Anniversary: 1829 – Patent is issued for "typographer" which becomes the typewriter

Born Today: 1888 – Raymond Chandler - author

Motivation: "When we put our problems in God's hands, he puts His peace in our hearts." – Unknown

Battle's Bullet: My prayer is you will receive comfort and peace from the Holy Spirit and be examples to others in dealing with uncertainty, lack of control, and the unbridled emotions of others.

Personal Observances:
_____
_____
_____

July  24

Stand Firm

Inspiration:	**Philippians 4:1** - Therefore, my brothers and sisters, you whom I love and long for, my joy and crown, **stand firm** in the Lord in this way, dear friends!
National Day:	National Drive-Thru Day
Anniversary:	1946 – Test Baker nuclear test on Bikini Island
Born Today:	1897 – Amelia Earhardt - aviator
Motivation:	"God's peace is not the calm after the storm, it is the steadfastness during it." – Dr. Michelle Bengston
Battle's Bullet:	God is always with me and provides me the strength I need in every situation.

Personal Observances:
_____
_____
_____

July 25

Wisdom

Inspiration:	**Proverbs 19:8** - The one who gets **wisdom** loves life; the one who cherishes understanding will soon prosper.
National Day:	National Hire a Veteran Day
Anniversary:	1868 – US Congress forms Wyoming territory
Born Today:	1894 – Walter Brennan - actor
Motivation:	"Common sense is not a gift. It is a punishment, because you have to deal with everyone who doesn't have it." – Funnyclub
Battle's Bullet:	Conventional wisdom is seeing what we perceive in front of us. I would submit what we see is filtered by what is behind our eyes in our attitudes.

Personal Observances:

_____
_____
_____

July  26

Perseverance

Inspiration: **James 1:12** - Blessed is the one who perseveres under trial because, having stood the test, that person will receive the crown of life that the Lord has promised to those who **love** him.

National Day: National Aunts and Uncles Day

Anniversary: 1775 – US Postal Service established by the Second Continental Congress

Born Today: 1858 – Edward M. House – political advisor

Motivation: "The struggle you're in today is developing the strength you need for tomorrow. Don't Give Up!" – Unknown

Battle's Bullet: Discarded dreams, lost opportunities, and a future without positive contributions, is the future of a person who discontinues persevering through trials.

Personal Observances:
_____
_____
_____

July 27

Trustworthy - Trust

Inspiration: **Psalm 32:10** - Many are the woes of the wicked, but the Lord's unfailing love surrounds the one who **trust**s in him.

National Day: National Love is Kind Day

Anniversary: 1940 – Bugs Bunny debuts in *Wild Hare* cartoon

Born Today: 1948 – Peggy Fleming – figure skater

Motivation: "Never trust someone who lies to you. Never lie to someone who trusts you." – Unknown

Battle's Bullet: If hindsight is 20-20, and experience is the best teacher, why won't the people who have neither listen to those who have both?

Personal Observances:
_____
_____
_____

July  28

Truth

Inspiration: **Galatians 4:16** - Have I now become your enemy by telling you the **truth**?

National Day: Buffalo Soldiers Day

Anniversary: 1868 – 14th Amendment to the U.S. Constitution takes force

Born Today: 1929 – Jacqueline Kennedy Onassis – First Lady

Motivation: "Truth exists; only lies are invented." – George Braque

Battle's Bullet: Using half-truths as deception is as old as time itself. Adam and Eve were both deceived by the serpent in the Garden of Eden.

Personal Observances:
_____
_____
_____

July 29

Victorious

Inspiration: **Revelation 2:26** - To the one who is **victorious** and does my will to the end, I will give authority over the nations—

National Day: National Chicken Wing Day

Anniversary: 1958 – NASA established

Born Today: 1937 – Charles Schwab - investments

Motivation: "A man is not measured by how much he can take and stand but by how fast he regains once fallen." – George S. Patton

Battle's Bullet: Successfully completing responsibilities will increase our confidence for further achievements.

Personal Observances:
_____
_____
_____

July 30

Thankful

Inspiration: **Psalm 100:4** - Enter his gates with **thanksgiving** and his courts with praise; give thanks to him and praise his name.

National Day: National Father-in-Law Day

Anniversary: 1872 – Mahlon Loomis issued patent for wireless telegraphy

Born Today: 1863 – Henry Ford – automotive leader

Motivation: "Reflect upon your present blessings, of which every man has plenty; not on your past misfortunes, of which all men have some." – Charles Dickens

Battle's Bullet: What you think is what you feel. THINK POSITIVELY and BE THANKFUL for what you have!

Personal Observances:

___
___
___

July 31

Good Cheer

Inspiration: **Proverbs 15:13** - A happy heart makes the face **cheer**ful, but heartache crushes the spirit.

National Day: National Mutt Day

Anniversary: 1620 – Pilgrims depart Leiden, Netherlands to England en route to America

Born Today: 1912 – Milton Freidman - economist

Motivation: "You can't have a good day with a bad attitude, and you can't have a bad day with a good attitude." – Positivelifetips.com

Battle's Bullet: People who are genuinely happy most of the time have a positive outlook on life.

Personal Observances:
___
___
___

AUGUST

August 1

Joy

Inspiration: **Psalm 67:4** - May the nations be glad and sing for **joy**, for you rule the peoples with equity and guide the nations of the earth.

National Day: Respect for Parents Day

Anniversary: 1996 – *A Game of Thrones* is first published

Born Today: 1770 – William Clark (Lewis &) - explorer

Motivation: "Joy is not the absence of suffering. It is the presence of God." – Robert Schuller

Battle's Bullet: May your journey through the course of life be joyous and every endeavor fruitful.

Personal Observances:
_____
_____
_____

August  2

Honor

Inspiration: **Romans 2:7** - To those who by persistence in doing good seek glory, **honor** and immortality, he will give eternal life.

National Day: National Coloring Book Day

Anniversary: 1876 – Wild Bill Hickok murdered in Deadwood, South Dakota

Born Today: 1834 – Frederic-Auguste Bartholdi – Statue of Liberty

Motivation: "Be honorable yourself if you wish to associate with honorable people." – Proverb

Battle's Bullet: Always keep your word.

Personal Observances:
_____
_____
_____

AUGUST 3

Heart

Inspiration: **Psalm 33:11** - But the plans of the Lord stand firm forever, the purposes of his **heart** through all generations.

National Day: National Watermelon Day

Anniversary: 1492 – Christopher Columbus sets sail on transatlantic voyage to discover the new world

Born Today: 1811 – Elisha Otis – elevator/inventor

Motivation: "No beauty shines brighter than that of a good heart." – Unknown

Battle's Bullet: Our attitude impacts everything in our life.

Personal Observances:
___
___
___

August 4

Hope

Inspiration:	**Proverbs 23:18** -There is surely a future **hope** for you, and your **hope** will not be cut off.
National Day:	National Coast Guard Day
Anniversary:	1862 – U.S. government collects its first income tax
Born Today:	1961 – President Barack Obama (44)
Motivation:	"In all things it is better to hope than to despair." – Johann Wolfgang Von Goethe
Battle's Bullet:	My Hope for you is that you don't delay recognizing what is there for you and that you, and everyone you touch, are positively impacted because of your decisions.

Personal Observances:
_____
_____
_____

August 5

Courage

Inspiration: **Acts 4:13** - When they saw the **courage** of Peter and John and realized that they were unschooled, ordinary men, they were astonished and they took note that these men had been with Jesus.

National Day: National Work Like a Dog Day

Anniversary: 1864 – Battle of Mobile Bay. Farragut orders, "Damn the torpedoes. Full speed ahead!"

Born Today: 1930 – Neil Armstrong – astronaut/first man to step foot on the moon

Motivation: "Courage is a love affair with the unknown." – Osho

Battle's Bullet: A positive attitude will also infect those around you and encourage people to support or join you in your effort.

Personal Observances:
_____
_____
_____

August 6

Act

Inspiration:	**Psalm 71:24** - My tongue will tell of your righteous **act**s all day long, for those who wanted to harm me have been put to shame and confusion.
National Day:	National Fresh Breath Day
Anniversary:	1945 – Atomic bomb dropped on Hiroshima
Born Today:	1911 – Lucille Ball - actress
Motivation:	"Act as if what you do makes a difference. It does." – William James
Battle's Bullet:	Be proactive. As the adage goes, take the bull by the horns.

Personal Observances:

_____
_____
_____

August 7

Fearless

Inspiration:	Ecclesiastes 8:13 - Yet because the wicked do **not fear** God, it will **not** go well with them, and their days will **not** lengthen like a shadow.
National Day:	Purple Heart Day
Anniversary:	1782 – George Washington creates the Purple Heart medal
Born Today:	1742 – Nathanael Greene – military leader
Motivation:	"We do not fear the unknown. We fear what we think we know about the unknown." – Teal Swan
Battle's Bullet:	"'Can't' never did anything." My Dad, Bill Battle.

Personal Observances:
_____
_____
_____

August 8

Humble

Inspiration:	**Proverbs 3:34** -He mocks proud mockers but shows favor to the **humble** and oppressed.
National Day:	National Dollar Day
Anniversary:	1786 – U.S. Congress adopts the dollar as monetary currency
Born Today:	1900 – Josephine Holt Bay – 1st woman to lead a NY stock exchange firm
Motivation:	"Humble enough to know I'm not better than anyone else and wise enough to know I'm different than the rest." – Unknown
Battle's Bullet:	It humbles me to hear people say my comments or writing encouraged their life.

Personal Observances:

_____
_____
_____

August 9

Faith - Faithful

Inspiration: 1 Peter 4:10 - Each of you should use whatever gift you have received to serve others, as **faith**ful stewards of God's grace in its various forms.

National Day: National Book Lovers Day

Anniversary: 1854 – Henry David Thoreau publishes "Walden"

Born Today: 1897 – Ralph Wyckoff - pioneer of X-ray crystallography

Motivation: "Increase your faith. Proclaim your faith. Let your faith show." – Russell M. Nelson

Battle's Bullet: Our level of faith in a controlling force beyond ourselves will substantially differentiate our ability to realize we aren't in control of what is occurring.

Personal Observances:
_____
_____
_____

August 10

Provision

Inspiration: 1 Timothy 6:17 - Command those who are rich in this present world not to be arrogant nor to put their hope in wealth, which is so uncertain, but to put their hope in God, who richly **provide**s us with everything for our enjoyment.

National Day: National Lazy Day

Anniversary: 1846 – Smithsonian Institute founded with funds from James Smithson

Born Today: 1874 – President Herbert Hoover (31)

Motivation: "The first years of man must make provision for the last." --Samuel Johnson

Battle's Bullet: As I have gotten older, it is easier to see God's provision in more and more and smaller and smaller things.

Personal Observances:
___
___
___

August 11

Mercy

Inspiration: Exodus 33:19 - And the Lord said, "I will cause all my goodness to pass in front of you, and I will proclaim my name, the Lord, in your presence. I will have **mercy** on whom I will have **mercy**, and I will have compassion on whom I will have compassion.

National Day: National Humor Day

Anniversary: 1942 – Actress Hedy Lamarr receives patent on wireless technology that influenced satellite and cell phone technologies

Born Today: 1921 – Alex Haley – author of *Roots*

Motivation: "Mercy, detached from Justice, grows unmerciful." - C.S. Lewis

Battle's Bullet: Our efforts in helping others may be the difference in outcomes beyond our comprehension.

Personal Observances:
_____
_____
_____

August 12

Forgiveness

Inspiration: Luke 17:4 – "Even if they sin against you seven times in a day and seven times come back to you saying 'I repent,' you must **forgive** them."

National Day: National Middle Child Day

Anniversary: 1908 – Ford builds the first Model-T automobile

Born Today: 1881 – Cecil B. DeMille - filmmaker

Motivation: "When someone is working hard to change, the worst thing you can do is hold them to their past. Forgive them and help them transform." – curiano quotes life

Battle's Bullet: Our opportunity to grow is in how we respond to failure. He forgives us, which entitles us to forgive ourselves.

Personal Observances:
_____
_____
_____

August 13

Grace

Inspiration:	**2 Corinthians 8:9** - For you know the **grace** of our Lord Jesus Christ, that though he was rich, yet for your sake he became poor, so that you through his poverty might become rich.
National Day:	International Left Handers Day
Anniversary:	1608 – John Smith's story of Jamestown's first days submitted for publication
Born Today:	1860 – Annie Oakley - sharpshooter
Motivation:	"Grace can warm a soul of worry and melt a heart of bitterness." – Rachel Wojo
Battle's Bullet:	Despite what we may experience, do we reflect on the gift that we are given daily in life and recognize things could always be worse?

Personal Observances:

_____
_____
_____

August 14

Love

Inspiration: **Psalm 51:1** - Have mercy on me, O God, according to your unfailing **love**; according to your great compassion blot out my transgressions.

National Day: National V-J Day

Anniversary: 1945 – VJ Day

Born Today: 1851 – Doc Holliday – Old West legendary figure

Motivation: "Lord, grant that I might not so much seek to be loved as to love." – St. Francis of Assisi

Battle's Bullet: Tell your loved ones you love them. Invest time with them because relationships are the most important thing in life.

Personal Observances:
_____
_____
_____

August  15

Rejoice

Inspiration: **Proverbs 23:24** - The father of a righteous child has great joy; a man who fathers a wise son **rejoice**s in him.

National Day: National Relaxation Day

Anniversary: 1971 – President Richard Nixon announces 90-day wage, price and rent freeze

Born Today: 1924 – Phyllis Schlafly – political activist

Motivation: "It is cheerful to God when you rejoice or laugh from the bottom of your heart." – Martin Luther King Jr.

Battle's Bullet: Pursuing our dreams instills enthusiasm and energy into all of our efforts, which increase their impact.

Personal Observances:
___
___
___

August  16

Adversity – Trials - Obstacles

Inspiration: Isaiah 57:14 - And it will be said: "Build up, build up, prepare the road! Remove the **obstacle**s out of the way of my people."

National Day: National Roller Coaster Day

Anniversary: 1896 – Gold first discovered in the Klondike

Born Today: 1862 – Amos Alonzo Stagg – football coach

Motivation: "People striving, being knocked down, and coming back, that's what builds character. I've seen very little character in players who never had to face adversity." – Tom Landry

Battle's Bullet: Our come back from adversity will determine the way it will impact our future.

Personal Observances:
_____
_____
_____

August 17

Encouragement

Inspiration:	**Philippians 2:1-3** - Therefore if you have any **encouragement** from being united with Christ, if any comfort from his love, if any common sharing in the Spirit, if any tenderness and compassion, then make my joy complete by being like-minded, having the same love, being one in spirit and of one mind. Do nothing out of selfish ambition or vain conceit. Rather, in humility value others above yourselves,
National Day:	National Non-Profits Day
Anniversary:	1939 – *Wizard of Oz* opens at Loews Capital Theatre in New York
Born Today:	1786 – Davy Crockett – statesman/Alamo defender/legend
Motivation:	"Faith tells me no matter what lies ahead of me, God is already there." – ibelieve.com
Battle's Bullet:	We should lift people with encouragement rather than depress them with discouragement.

Personal Observances:

_____
_____
_____

August 18

Endurance

Inspiration: **2 Corinthians 6:4** - Rather, as servants of God we commend ourselves in every way: in great **endurance**; in troubles, hardships and distresses;

National Day: National Fajita Day

Anniversary: 1956 – Elvis Presley's *Hound Dog* and *Don't Be Cruel* both hit #1 on the hit charts

Born Today: 1774 – Meriweather Lewis (Clark) - explorer

Motivation: "There are no shortcuts to endurance. You have to train yourself to make peace with the long route every day, and do it, and love where it is taking you." – Unknown

Battle's Bullet: When I looked back after my son's passing, I could see instances where God had prepared me to endure it and survive.

Personal Observances:
_____
_____
_____

August 19

Example

Inspiration: **1 Corinthians 10:6** - Now these things occurred as **example**s to keep us from setting our hearts on evil things as they did.

National Day: National Soft Ice Cream Day

Anniversary: 1909 – Indianapolis racetrack opens

Born Today: 1946 – President Bill Clinton (42)

1871 – Orville Wright – first to fly

Motivation: "The three most important ways to lead people are: by example…by example. By example." – Albert Schweitzer

Battle's Bullet: Be an example to others to imbue them with confidence for their life journey.

Personal Observances:
_____
_____
_____

August 20

Grow

Inspiration:	**Ephesians 4:15** - Instead, speaking the truth in love, we will **grow** to become in every respect the mature body of him who is the head, that is, Christ.
National Day:	National Cousins Day
Anniversary:	1866 – President Andrew Johnson declares Civil War is officially over
Born Today:	1833 – President Benjamin Harrison (23)
Motivation:	"Spiritual growth is the only growth that pays dividends over lifetimes." – Allan Martin Osman
Battle's Bullet:	While waiting for an opportunity:

- Be Positive
- Be Ready
- Focus on what you can control
- Accept what you can't control

Personal Observances:

_____
_____
_____

LIFE'S DAILY TREASURE

August 21

Overcomer

Inspiration: **John 16:33** - "I have told you these things, so that in me you may have peace. In this world you will have trouble. But take heart! I have **overcome** the world."

National Day: National Senior Citizens Day

Anniversary: 1888 – Inventor William Seward Burroughs patents the adding machine

Born Today: 1906 – Friz Freleng - animator

Motivation: "Challenges are what make life interesting. Overcoming them is what makes them meaningful." – Joshua J., Marine

Battle's Bullet: Even if a situation looks hopeless or impossible, we should ALWAYS do the best that we can. Who knows when that extra effort may result in an extraordinary result?

Personal Observances:
___
___
___

August  22

Patience

Inspiration: Isaiah 7:13 - Then Isaiah said, "Hear now, you house of David! Is it not enough to try the **patience** of humans? Will you try the **patience** of my God also?

National Day: National Tooth Fairy Day

Anniversary: 1902 – President Theodore Roosevelt is the first president to ride in a car

Born Today: 1920 – Ray Bradbury - author

Motivation: "Patience means trusting God even when the circumstances haven't changed yet." – Unknown

Battle's Bullet: Like many other characteristics essential to our success and happiness, patience is one that we are not born with but hopefully will learn through the rigors of experience.

Personal Observances:
___
___
___

August  23

Peace

Inspiration:	**Proverbs 29:17** - Discipline your children, and they will give you **peace**; they will bring you the delights you desire.
National Day:	National Sponge Cake Day
Anniversary:	1947 – First Little League World Series game in Williamsport, Pennsylvania
Born Today:	1978 – Kobe Bryant - basketball
Motivation:	"Don't let the behavior of others destroy your inner peace." – Dalai Lama
Battle's Bullet:	When our heart is in the right place, and we're fulfilling our purpose, peace is our reward.

Personal Observances:

_____
_____
_____

August  24

Stand Firm

Inspiration:	Mark 13:13 - Everyone will hate you because of me, but the one who **stands firm** to the end will be saved.
National Day:	National Peach Pie and Waffle Day
Anniversary:	1857 – One of the worst economic panics in U.S. history begins
Born Today:	1897 – Fred Rose – music executive
Motivation:	"True loyalty is that quality of service that grows under adversity and expands in defeat. Any street urchin can shout applause in victory, but it takes character to stand fast in defeat. One is noise – the other, loyalty." – Fielding A. Yost
Battle's Bullet:	Will we quit at the first sign of trouble, or will we stand and face it to succeed?

Personal Observances:

_____
_____
_____

August 25

Wisdom

Inspiration: **Proverbs 4:6-7** - Do not forsake **wisdom**, and she will protect you; love her, and she will watch over you. The beginning of **wisdom** is this: Get **wisdom**. Though it cost all you have, get understanding.

National Day: National Kiss and Make Up Day

Anniversary: 1952 – Puerto Rico becomes a U.S. commonwealth

Born Today: 1836 – Bret Harte - Author

Motivation: "Lessons in life will be repeated until they are learned." – Frank Sonnenberg

Battle's Bullet: A wise man once asked me, "Do you remember what you worried about three years ago?" When I thought back, I couldn't remember.

Personal Observances:
___
___
___

August 26

Perseverance

Inspiration: **2 Thessalonians 3:5** - May the Lord direct your hearts into God's love and Christ's **perseverance**.

National Day: National Dog Day

Anniversary: 1939 – First Major League baseball telecast; Reds beat Dodgers.

Born Today: 1901 – Maj. Gen. Maxwell Taylor - military

Motivation: "Most of the important things in the world have been accomplished by people who kept on trying when there seemed to be no hope at all." – Dale Carnegie

Battle's Bullet: People are willing to take risks in life because they understand that is the only way they are ever going to change their circumstances.

Personal Observances:
___
___
___

August 27

Trustworthy - Trust

Inspiration: **Psalm 40:4** - Blessed is the one who **trust**s in the Lord, who does not look to the proud, to those who turn aside to false gods.

National Day: National Just Because Day

Anniversary: 1928 – Kellogg-Briand pact condemns war as solution to international problems

Born Today: 1908 – President Lyndon Johnson (36)

Motivation: "Never be afraid to trust an unknown future to a known God." – Corrie Ten Boom

Battle's Bullet: If we prove that we are trustworthy, we will elevate our opportunity for success significantly.

Personal Observances:

_____
_____
_____

August 28

Truth

Inspiration:	**1 John 1:8** - If we claim to be without sin, we deceive ourselves and the **truth** is not in us.
National Day:	National Red Wine Day
Anniversary:	1963 – Martin Luther King Jr. delivers his "I Have a Dream Speech" in Washington
Born Today:	1917 – Jack Kirby - cartoonist
Motivation:	"Anyone who doesn't take truth seriously in small matters cannot be trusted in large ones either." – Albert Einstein
Battle's Bullet:	Not only will lies damage people for a long time, but they also inflict injury more rapidly than the truth supplies betterment.

Personal Observances:
_____
_____
_____

August 29

Victorious

Inspiration: **Zechariah 9:9** - Rejoice greatly, Daughter Zion! Shout, Daughter Jerusalem! See, your king comes to you, righteous and **victorious**, lowly and riding on a donkey, on a colt, the foal of a donkey.

National Day: National Chop Suey Day

Anniversary: 1758 – New Jersey legislature creates the first Indian reservation

Born Today: 1958 – Michael Jackson - entertainer

Motivation: "Only he who gives up is defeated. Everyone else is victorious." – Paulo Coelho

Battle's Bullet: Vision+ Risk+ Action+ Focus+ Dedication+ Persistence+ Every day= Victory

Personal Observances:
___
___
___

August 30

Thankful

Inspiration: **Psalm 95:2** - Let us come before him with **thanksgiving** and extol him with music and song.

National Day: National Grief Awareness Day

Anniversary: 1967 – Thurgood Marshall becomes first African-American Supreme Court Justice

Born Today: 1930 – Warren Buffet - investor

Motivation: "The more you thank life, the more life gives you to be thankful for." – gratitudehabitat.com

Battle's Bullet: Have you taken a minute lately to be thankful for something that has improved your life because of improvements hastened by the free enterprise system?

Personal Observances:
_____
_____
_____

August  31

Good Cheer

Inspiration: **Proverbs 15:15** - All the days of the oppressed are wretched, but the **cheer**ful heart has a continual feast.

National Day: National Matchmaker Day

Anniversary: 1897 – Thomas Edison patents Kinetoscope -- the first device producing moving pictures

Born Today: 1897 – Frederic March - actor

Motivation: "We can complain because rose bushes have thorns or rejoice because thorn bushes have roses." – President Abraham Lincoln

Battle's Bullet: Conquering Life's Course means our life was fruitful and positively impacted and served others, and we did not waste on frivolity.

Personal Observances:
_____
_____
_____

SEPTEMBER

September 1

Joy

Inspiration: **Proverbs 10:28** - The prospect of the righteous is **joy**, but the hopes of the wicked come to nothing.

National Day: National Chicken Boy's Day

Anniversary: 1752 – The Liberty Bell arrives in Philadelphia

Born Today: 1875 – Edgar Rice Burroughs - author

Motivation: "Find joy in the journey." – Thomas S. Monson

Battle's Bullet: May you enjoy where you are every day and make every day fruitful.

Personal Observances:
___
___
___

September 2

Honor

Inspiration:	**Revelation 4:11** – "You are worthy, our Lord and God, to receive glory and **honor** and power, for you created all things, and by your will they were created and have their being."
National Day:	National V-J Day
Anniversary:	1945 – V-J Day - World War II
Born Today:	1948 – Christa McAuliffe – educator/astronaut
Motivation:	"An honorable man restores the dignity of others." --sevenly.org
Battle's Bullet:	A job well done is Always rewarded in some way.

Personal Observances:
_____
_____
_____

September 3

Heart

Inspiration: **Hebrews 12:3** - Consider him who endured such opposition from sinners, so that you will not grow weary and lose **heart**.

National Day: U. S. Bowling League Day

Anniversary: 1838 – Frederick Douglass escapes slavery

Born Today: 1913 – Alan Ladd – actor

Motivation: "We enter Heaven not with healed hearts but with His heart." – Touching Hearts

Battle's Bullet: I strive to be a positive example to others based on the model Jesus provided us.

Personal Observances:
_____
_____
_____

September 4

Hope

Inspiration: **Romans 5:2b-5** - And we boast in the hope of the glory of God. Not only so, but we also glory in our sufferings, because we know that suffering produces perseverance; perseverance, character; and character, hope. And hope does not put us to shame, because God's love has been poured out into our hearts through the Holy Spirit, who has been given to us.

National Day: National Wildlife Day

Anniversary: 1882 – Thomas Edison's first large scale test of the electric light bulb

Born Today: 1918 – Paul Harvey – radio commentator

Motivation: "Hope is the only thing stronger than fear." – Suzanne Collins

Battle's Bullet: Don't fall for the head fake of false Hope.

Personal Observances:

_____
_____
_____

September 5

Courage

Inspiration: **1 Corinthians 16:13** - Be on your guard; stand firm in the faith; be **courage**ous; be strong.

National Day: National Cheese Pizza Day

Anniversary: 1836 – Sam Houston elected the first president of The Republic of Texas

Born Today: 1902 – Darryl F. Zanuck – film executive

Motivation: "A single feat of daring can alter the whole conception of what is possible." – Graham Greene

Battle's Bullet: Success breeds confidence that we will achieve further success.

Personal Observances:
_____
_____
_____

September 6

Act

Inspiration: Isaiah 5:16 - But the Lord Almighty will be exalted by his justice, and the holy God will be proved holy by his righteous **act**s.

National Day: National Read a Book Day

Anniversary: 1620 – The Mayflower departs Plymouth for the New World

Born Today: 1890 – Claire Chennault – military/Flying Tigers

Motivation: "Do every act of your life as if it were your last." – Marcus Aurelius

Battle's Bullet: When in doubt, act. There is rarely profit in paralysis.

Personal Observances:
_____
_____
_____

September 7

Fearless

Inspiration:	**Isaiah 54:4** - "Do **not** be afraid; you will **not** be put to shame. Do **not fear** disgrace; you will **not** be humiliated. You will forget the shame of your youth and remember no more the reproach of your widowhood.
National Day:	National Beer Lover's Day
Anniversary:	1888 – First baby incubator is used at hospital in New York
Born Today:	1936 – Buddy Holly - singer
Motivation:	"Without God I am hopeless, with God I am fearless." – picturequotes.com
Battle's Bullet:	Forward, always move ahead.

Personal Observances:

_____
_____
_____

SEPTEMBER 8

Humble

Inspiration:	**Psalm 147:6** - The Lord sustains the **humble** but casts the wicked to the ground.
National Day:	National Ampersand Day
Anniversary:	1966 – *Star Trek* premieres on television
Born Today:	1828 – Joshua Chamberlain – theologian/military
Motivation:	"True humility is not thinking less of yourself; it is thinking of yourself less." – Rick Warren
Battle's Bullet:	There is no way to know how many or which people or how long our example might benefit others.

Personal Observances:

_____
_____
_____

September 9

Faith - Faithful

Inspiration: 2 Timothy 4:7 - I have fought the good fight, I have finished the race, I have kept the **faith**.

National Day: National Teddy Bear Day

Anniversary: 1956 – Elvis Presley appears on *The Ed Sullivan Show* for the first time

Born Today: 1890 – (Col.) Harland Sanders - KFC

Motivation: "Faith is to believe what you do not see; the reward of this faith is to see what you believe." – St. Augustine

Battle's Bullet: My faith enables me to live without fear of what may happen here and look forward to what will happen for eternity.

Personal Observances:
_____
_____
_____

September  10

Provision

Inspiration: **Psalm 18:36** - You **provide** a broad path for my feet, so that my ankles do not give way.

National Day: National TV Dinner Day

Anniversary: 1608 – John Smith elected president of the Jamestown colony

Born Today: 1929 – Arnold Palmer - golf

Motivation: "God will make a way when there seems to be no way. He works in ways we cannot see, He will make a way for me." – Unknown

Battle's Bullet: Overcome the perception we can't make a difference in improving the future; Sydney Smith said, "It is the greatest of all mistakes to do nothing. Do what you can."

Personal Observances:
___
___
___

SEPTEMBER 11

Mercy

Inspiration:	Micah 7:18 -Who is a God like you, who pardons sin and forgives the transgression of the remnant of his inheritance? You do not stay angry forever but delight to show **mercy**.
National Day:	Patriot Day and National Day of Service and Remembrance
Anniversary:	2001 – 9/11 attacks on New York City, Washington D.C. and Shanksville, Pennsylvania
Born Today:	1862 – O. Henry (William Sydney Porter) - author
Motivation:	"Where mercy, love, and pity dwell, there God is dwelling too." – William Blake
Battle's Bullet:	God can turn loss and failure into service and success.

Personal Observances:

_____
_____
_____

September 12

Forgiveness

Inspiration: Mark 11:25 - And when you stand praying, if you hold anything against anyone, **forgive** them, so that your Father in heaven may **forgive** you your sins."

National Day: National Day of Encouragement

Anniversary: 1958 – U. S. Supreme Court orders integration of Little Rock, Arkansas schools

Born Today: 1913 – Jesse Owens - athlete and Olympian

Motivation: "Relationships get stronger when both are willing to understand mistakes and forgive each other." – kushandwizdom

Battle's Bullet: Remember: We learn more from our mistakes than our successes.

Personal Observances:
___
___
___

September 13

Grace

Inspiration: Titus 3:7 - so that, having been justified by his **grace**, we might become heirs having the hope of eternal life.

National Day: Uncle Sam Day

Anniversary: 1969 – *Scooby-Doo Where are You?* cartoon debuts on television

Born Today: 1860 – John J. Pershing – military

Motivation: "I don't know exactly what's next, but I am stepping forward with grit anchored in Grace." – Julie Graham

Battle's Bullet: If we cherish and utilize our gifts positively and for others' benefit, might we receive more opportunities and responsibilities?

Personal Observances:
___
___
___

September 14

Love

Inspiration:	1 John 2:15 - Do not **love** the world or anything in the world. If anyone **love**s the world, **love** for the Father is not in them.
National Day:	National Crème Filled Doughnut Day
Anniversary:	1814 – Francis Scott Key writes *The Star-Spangled Banner* after witnessing Fort McHenry attack.
Born Today:	1914 – Clayton Moore – actor, *The Lone Ranger*
Motivation:	"Lord Jesus help me to love the way you love." – zebsparkinglot
Battle's Bullet:	God loved me before I was even born and continues to provide for me and encourage me that regardless of what happens in this life, He has a place for me with Him in eternity.

Personal Observances:

_____
_____
_____

September 15

Rejoice

Inspiration: **Zephaniah 3:17** - The Lord your God is with you, the Mighty Warrior who saves. He will take great delight in you; in his love he will no longer rebuke you, but will **rejoice** over you with singing."

National Day: National Tackle Kids Cancer Day

Anniversary: 1949 – *The Lone Ranger* premieres on ABC-TV

Born Today: 1857 – President William Howard Taft (27)

Motivation: "Begin to recognize prosperity everywhere, and rejoice in it." – Louise Hay

Battle's Bullet: I strive to grow spiritually daily.

Personal Observances:
___
___
___

September 16

Adversity – Trials - Obstacles

Inspiration:	**1 Thessalonians 3:3** - so that no one would be unsettled by these **trials**. For you know quite well that we are destined for them.
National Day:	Mayflower Day
Anniversary:	1782 – Great seal of the U.S. is used for the first time
Born Today:	1875 – J. C. Penney – retailer
Motivation:	"A challenge only becomes an obstacle when you bow to it." – Unknown
Battle's Bullet:	When trials happen, I pray fervently to learn the lesson or lessons that I am supposed to learn, not to have to suffer a second time to learn one lesson.

Personal Observances:
_____
_____
_____

September 17

Encouragement

Inspiration: **Acts 11:23** - When he arrived and saw what the grace of God had done, he was glad and **encourage**d them all to remain true to the Lord with all their hearts.

National Day: Constitution Day and Citizenship Day

Anniversary: 1787 – U.S. Constitution adopted

Born Today: 1923 – Hank Williams - music

Motivation: "Faith tells me no matter what lies ahead of me, God is already there." – ibelieve.com

Battle's Bullet: We never know the number of people or the amount of impact we may have with a timely word of encouragement to others.

Personal Observances:
_____
_____
_____

September 18

Endurance

Inspiration:	**Titus 2:2** - Teach the older men to be temperate, worthy of respect, self-controlled, and sound in faith, in love and in **endurance**.
National Day:	Air Force Birthday
Anniversary:	1793 – President George Washington lays the cornerstone for the U.S. Capitol
Born Today:	1770 – Joseph Story – U.S. Supreme Court
Motivation:	"I have endured. I have been broken. I know hardship. I have lost myself. But here I stand still moving forward, growing stronger each day. I will never forget the harsh lessons of my life. They make me stronger." – facebook.com/Daveswordsofwisdom
Battle's Bullet:	Facing difficulties does build endurance and resilience, which increases our confidence to absorb the next threat we encounter.

Personal Observances:

_____
_____
_____

September 19

Example

Inspiration: **1 Peter 5:3** - not lording it over those entrusted to you, but being **example**s to the flock.

National Day: National Talk Like a Pirate Day

Anniversary: 1947 – Jackie Robinson named Major League Baseball "Rookie of the Year"

Born Today: 1965 – Sunita Williams – American astronaut

Motivation: "Leadership is not a position or a title. It is an example." – Unknown

Battle's Bullet: The best leadership is by example.

Personal Observances:

_____
_____
_____

September 20

Grow

Inspiration: **Isaiah 40:28** - Do you not know? Have you not heard? The Lord is the everlasting God, the Creator of the ends of the earth. He will not **grow** tired or weary, and his understanding no one can fathom.

National Day: National Pepperoni Pizza

Anniversary: 1954 – First run of FORTRAN computer program

Born Today: 1878 – Upton Sinclair - author

Motivation: "If you want light to come into your life, you need to stand where it is shining." – Guy Finley

Battle's Bullet: If we haven't experienced a setback in business, we haven't taken or been allowed to grow outside our comfort zone.

Personal Observances:
_____
_____
_____

September 21

Overcomer

Inspiration: 1 John 4:4 - You, dear children, are from God and have **overcome** them, because the one who is in you is greater than the one who is in the world.

National Day: National Pecan Cookie Day

Anniversary: 1780 – Benedict Arnold commits treason giving the British plans to West Point

Born Today: 1950 – Bill Murray - actor

Motivation: "It is amazing what you can do when you don't know what you can't do." - Unknown

Battle's Bullet: We choose whether to declare ourselves a victim of life or an overcomer of whatever life deals us.

Personal Observances:
___
___
___

September 22

Patience

Inspiration: **Romans 2:4** - Or do you show contempt for the riches of his kindness, forbearance and **patience**, not realizing that God's kindness is intended to lead you to repentance?

National Day: National Ice Cream Day

Anniversary: 1776 – 21-year-old Nathan Hale hung after saying, "My only regret is I have but one life to give to my country."

Born Today: 1927 – Tommy Lasorda - baseball

Motivation: "Patience is the calm acceptance that things can happen in a different order than the one you have in mind." – David G. Allen

Battle's Bullet: Even after we learn patience, we must exercise patience regularly for it to become a part of our character.

Personal Observances:
___
___
___

September 23

Peace

Inspiration: **Isaiah 53:5** - But he was pierced for our transgressions, he was crushed for our iniquities; the punishment that brought us **peace** was on him, and by his wounds we are healed.

National Day: National Great American Pot Pie Day

Anniversary: 1806 – Lewis and Clark return to St. Louis from two-plus year Northwest expedition

Born Today: 1930 – Ray Charles - music

Motivation: "Peace is not the absence of trouble, but the presence of Christ." – Sheila Walsh

Battle's Bullet: Hope in self for peace is futile.

Personal Observances:

_____

_____

_____

September 24

Stand Firm

Inspiration:	**Matthew 10:22** - You will be hated by everyone because of me, but the one who **stands firm** to the end will be saved.
National Day:	National Punctuation Day
Anniversary:	1952 – First KFC franchise opens
Born Today:	1755 – John Marshall – Chief Justice, U.S. Supreme Court
Motivation:	"Be on your guard; stand firm in the faith; be men of courage; be strong." – Paul letter to the church in Corinth. - 1 Corinthians 16:13
Battle's Bullet:	Our forefathers, who suffered mightily through pandemic, depression, and world wars, have shown us the way, and we stand on their shoulders.

Personal Observances:

_____
_____
_____

September 25

Wisdom

Inspiration: **Proverbs 3:13** - Blessed are those who find **wisdom**, those who gain understanding,

National Day: National Quesadilla Day

Anniversary: 1926 – Henry Ford begins 8-hour, 5-days-a-week work schedule

Born Today: 1929 – Barbara Walters – journalist/television

Motivation: "To expect the unexpected shows a thoroughly modern intellect." – Oscar Wilde

Battle's Bullet: Until recently, each generation's contributions provided solid foundations of wisdom to make deliberative decisions based on precedent, knowledge, and compassion.

Personal Observances:
___
___
___

September 26

Perseverance

Inspiration:	**Philippians 3:13b-15** - But **on**e thing I do: Forgetting what is behind and straining toward what is ahead, I **press on** toward the goal to win the prize for which God has called me heavenward in Christ Jesus.
National Day:	National Hunting and Fishing Day
Anniversary:	1960 – First presidential debate on television between John Kennedy and Richard Nixon
Born Today:	1981 – Serena Williams - tennis
Motivation:	"With ordinary talent and extraordinary perseverance, all things are attainable." – Thomas Powell Buxton
Battle's Bullet:	Despite persisting when we face adversity, we will not always succeed. We must persevere through it and beyond.

Personal Observances:

_____
_____
_____

September 27

Trustworthy - Trust

Inspiration: Psalm 56:11 – in God I **trust** and am not afraid. What can man do to me?

National Day: National Chocolate Milk Day

Anniversary: 1908 – First Ford Model-T produced in Detroit

Born Today: 1722 – Samuel Adams – American Founding Father

Motivation: "God never disappoints anyone who places trust in Him." Basilea Schlink

Battle's Bullet: In reality, we should trust our experience, which tells us that we should always verify what we see to determine if it is real or not.

Personal Observances:
_____
_____
_____

September 28

Truth

Inspiration:	**Proverbs 12:19** - **Truth**ful lips endure forever, but a lying tongue lasts only a moment.
National Day:	National Good Neighbor Day
Anniversary:	1542 – Juan Rodriguez Cabrillo discovers California and claims it for Spain
Born Today:	1852 – Captain Bill McDonald – Texas Rangers
Motivation:	"Seek not greatness, but seek truth and you will find both." – Horace Mann
Battle's Bullet:	People are having a harder and harder time discerning **the** truth from conflicting information.

Personal Observances:
_____
_____
_____

SEPTEMBER 29

Victorious

Inspiration: Revelation 3:21 - To the one who is **victorious**, I will give the right to sit with me on my throne, just as I was **victorious** and sat down with my Father on his throne.

National Day: National Coffee Day

Anniversary: 1948 – *Hamlet* movie directed and starring Laurence Olivier debuts

Born Today: 1907 – Gene Autry – music/TV/movies

Motivation: "The secret of all victory lies in the organization of the non-obvious." – Marcus Aurelius

Battle's Bullet: Strive for excellence in ALL things. You may not achieve it, but will accomplish much more than you will with an ordinary effort.

Personal Observances:
___
___
___

September 30

Thankful

Inspiration:	**Psalm 69:30** - I will praise God's name in song and glorify him with **thanksgiving**.
National Day:	National Love People Day
Anniversary:	1935 – Hoover Dam dedicated by President Franklin Roosevelt
Born Today:	1924 – Truman Capote - author
Motivation:	"The hardest arithmetic to master is that which enables us to count our blessings." – Eric Hoffer
Battle's Bullet:	Thankfully, we who are blessed to live in the United States have the opportunity to overcome any shortcomings in our birth and excel based on individual determination and effort.

Personal Observances:

_____
_____
_____

OCTOBER

OCTOBER  1

Joy

Inspiration:	Galatians 5:22 - But the fruit of the Spirit is love, **joy**, peace, forbearance, kindness, goodness, faithfulness,
National Day:	National Hair Day
Anniversary:	1880 – John Phillip Sousa begins as director of U.S. Marine Corps Band
Born Today:	1924 – President Jimmy Carter (39)
Motivation:	"I find joy in every day, not because life is always good, but God is." – dandelionquotes.com
Battle's Bullet:	May you discover your calling, redirect your route, enjoy the trip, and celebrate your triumphant arrival at the safe harbor you set out to reach.

Personal Observances:

_____
_____
_____

October 2

Honor

Inspiration: Psalm 62:7 - My salvation and my **honor** depend on God; he is my mighty rock, my refuge.

National Day: National Custodial Worker's Recognition Day

Anniversary: 1950 – First Charlie Brown comic by Charles M. Schulz. Became *Peanuts*.

Born Today: 1890 – Groucho Marx - comedian

Motivation: "If you can't honor your words, don't use them." --tightentheslack.com

Battle's Bullet: Always be sincere.

Personal Observances:
_____
_____
_____

October  3

Heart

Inspiration: **2 Corinthians 4:16** - Therefore we do not lose **heart**. Though outwardly we are wasting away, yet inwardly we are being renewed day by day.

National Day: National Boyfriend Day

Anniversary: 1913 – U.S. Federal income tax signed into law by President Woodrow Wilson

Born Today: 1451 – Christopher Columbus - explorer

Motivation: "May your heart always be joyful. May your song always be sung." – Bob Dylan

Battle's Bullet: My hope is you can learn from my ideas without making the errors I made to understand them.

Personal Observances:
_____
_____
_____

October  4

Hope

Inspiration: 1 Corinthians 13:13 - And now these three remain: faith, **hope** and love. But the greatest of these is love.

National Day: National Taco Day

Anniversary: 1854 – First political speech by Abraham Lincoln at Illinois State Fair

Born Today: 1822 – President Rutherford B. Hayes (19)

Motivation: "Where there is hope, there is faith. Where there is faith, miracles happen." – Unknown

Battle's Bullet: I hope that your path is forward and paved with the assurance that comes from well-thought-out decisions.

Personal Observances:
_____
_____
_____

October  5

Courage

Inspiration: **Ezekiel 22:14** - Will your **courage** endure or your hands be strong in the day I deal with you? I the Lord have spoken, and I will do it.

National Day: National Do Something Nice Day

Anniversary: 1947 – First televised address from the White House by President Truman

Born Today: 1829 – President Chester A. Arthur (21)
1703 – Jonathan Edwards - pastor

Motivation: "Courage is grace under pressure." – Ernest Hemmingway

Battle's Bullet: If we want to "get ahead," we always have to do our very best in everything we attempt.

Personal Observances:
_____
_____
_____

October 6

Act

Inspiration:	**Galatians 6:4** - Each one should test their own **act**ions. Then they can take pride in themselves alone, without comparing themselves to someone else,
National Day:	National Coaches' Day
Anniversary:	1889 – Thomas Edison presents his first motion picture
Born Today:	1846 – George Westinghouse – engineer and entrepreneur
Motivation:	"Be great in act as you have been in thought." – William Shakespeare
Battle's Bullet:	We never know when someone is looking to us for that example, which means that we should always act as if that moment is our example for others.

Personal Observances:

_____
_____
_____

October 7

Fearless

Inspiration: **Ephesians 6:19** - Pray also for me, that whenever I speak, words may be given me so that I will **fearless**ly make known the mystery of the gospel,

National Day: National Inner Beauty Day

Anniversary: 1963 – Nuclear Test Ban Treaty signed by President Kennedy

Born Today: 1955 – Yo-Yo Ma - music

Motivation: "Do one thing every day that scares you." – Eleanor Roosevelt

Battle's Bullet: We will make mistakes. Don't be afraid. It's not how many times we get knocked down in life that counts, but how many times we get back up.

Personal Observances:
___
___
___

October 8

Humble

Inspiration:	**Psalm 25:9** - He guides the **humble** in what is right and teaches them his way.
National Day:	National Touch Tag Day
Anniversary:	1918 – Sgt. Alvin York's Medal of Honor action in France
Born Today:	1890 – Eddie Rickenbacker – pilot and Medal of Honor recipient
Motivation:	"In a humble state, you'll learn better." – John Dooner
Battle's Bullet:	When we live without regretting missed opportunities, we can relax, knowing we achieved our destiny.

Personal Observances:
_____
_____
_____

October 9

Faith - Faithful

Inspiration: 1 Peter 1:21 - Through him you believe in God, who raised him from the dead and glorified him, and so your **faith** and hope are in God.

National Day: National Leif Erikson Day

Anniversary: 1865 – First underground oil pipeline is laid in Pennsylvania

Born Today: 1823 – Mary Ann Shadd Cary – publisher and suffragist

Motivation: "Faith expects from God what is beyond all expectation." – Andrew Murray

Battle's Bullet: My faith and hope in our Lord give me hope every day that regardless of what obstacles I face, He is there beside me to help me endure them.

Personal Observances:
_____
_____
_____

October  10

Provision

Inspiration:	**Romans 11:22** - Consider therefore the kindness and sternness of God: sternness to those who fell, but kindness to you, **provided** that you continue in his kindness. Otherwise, you also will be cut off.
National Day:	National Handbag Day
Anniversary:	1865 – John Wesley Hyatt patents the billiard ball
Born Today:	1900 – Helen Hayes - actress
Motivation:	"It's not that I'm so smart, it's just that I stay with problems longer." – Albert Einstein
Battle's Bullet:	God is always with me and provides for my every need.

Personal Observances:
___
___
___

October 11

Mercy

Inspiration: **2 Samuel 24:14** - David said to Gad, "I am in deep distress. Let us fall into the hands of the Lord, for his **mercy** is great; but do not let me fall into human hands."

National Day: General Pulaski Memorial Day

Anniversary: 1975 – *Saturday Night Live* premieres on television

Born Today: 1884 – Eleanor Roosevelt – First Lady

Motivation: "There are three things in the world that deserve no Mercy; hypocrisy, fraud, and tyranny." – Frederick W. Robertson

Battle's Bullet: Do you remember those individuals who gave you gifts that benefitted your life more than money?

Personal Observances:
___
___
___

October  12

Forgiveness

Inspiration:	Hebrews 5:4 - And no one takes this **honor** on himself, but he receives it when called by God, just as Aaron was.
National Day:	National Farmer's Day
Anniversary:	1492 – Christopher Columbus makes landfall in the New World
Born Today:	1912 – Doris Miller – first African-American Navy Cross recipient
Motivation:	"Never give up asking forgiveness from God. Your sins are not greater than God's mercy." --picturequotes.com
Battle's Bullet:	Forgiving others is one of the greatest gifts we can give ourselves because it frees our heart of anger.

Personal Observances:
___
___
___

OCTOBER 13

Grace

Inspiration:	**Hebrews 4:16** - Let us then approach God's throne of **grace** with confidence, so that we may receive mercy and find **grace** to help us in our time of need.
National Day:	Navy Birthday
Anniversary:	1792 – First edition of *The Old Farmer's Almanac* is published
Born Today:	1941 – Paul Simon - music
Motivation:	"Grace is when God gives us what we don't deserve. Mercy is when God doesn't give us what we deserve." – Winning Possibilities 2012
Battle's Bullet:	Each of us has different gifts that constitute a community positioned to help and support each other through difficult lifetimes.

Personal Observances:
_____
_____
_____

October  14

Love

Inspiration:	**Romans 8:28** - And we know that in all things God works for the good of those who **love** him, who have been called according to his purpose.
National Day:	National Dessert Day
Anniversary:	1884 – George Eastman patents paper-based photographic film
Born Today:	1890 – President Dwight Eisenhower (34)
Motivation:	"Life minus love equals zero." – Rick Warren
Battle's Bullet:	God always prepares us for where He is taking us, and He protects us throughout our life.

Personal Observances:
___
___
___

October  15

Rejoice

Inspiration: **Habakkuk 3:18** - yet I will **rejoice** in the Lord, I will be joyful in God my Savior.

National Day: National Pregnancy and Infant Loss Awareness Day

Anniversary: 1951 – *I Love Lucy* makes its television premiere

Born Today: 1924 – Lee Iacocca – automobile executive

Motivation: "It is both a privilege and a duty to rejoice in the Lord." – A.W. Pink

Battle's Bullet: We can't grow or positively impact anyone or anything with a negative attitude.

Personal Observances:
_____
_____
_____

October 16

Adversity – Trials - Obstacles

Inspiration: **Romans 16:17** - I urge you, brothers and sisters, to watch out for those who cause divisions and put **obstacle**s in your way that are contrary to the teaching you have learned. Keep away from them.

National Day: National Sports Day

Anniversary: 1923 – Disney cartoon studio opens.

Born Today: 1758 – Noah Webster - lexicographer

Motivation: "There is no education like adversity." – Benjamin Disraeli

Battle's Bullet: The pressure that results from adversity reveals our character.

Personal Observances:
_____
_____
_____

October  17

Encouragement

Inspiration: **Romans 1:12** - that is, that you and I may be mutually **encourage**d by each other's faith.

National Day: National Pasta Day

Anniversary: 1957 – *Jailhouse Rock* by Elvis Presley premieres

Born Today: 1915 – Arthur Miller – playwright

Motivation: "Be strong because things will get better. It may be stormy now, but it never rains forever."
--mydearvalentine.com

Battle's Bullet: When we encourage people to channel their energy into endeavors larger than themselves, we can help lift the human spirit for years to come.

Personal Observances:
___
___
___

OCTOBER 18

Endurance

Inspiration:	**Revelation 1:9** - I, John, your brother and companion in the suffering and kingdom and patient **endurance** that are ours in Jesus, was on the island of Patmos because of the word of God and the testimony of Jesus.
National Day:	National Legging Day
Anniversary:	1867 – Alaska purchase completed
Born Today:	1927 – George C. Scott - actor
Motivation:	"Getting back to basics is the simplest way to find calm in the chaos." - Unknown
Battle's Bullet:	When storms arise, people who set aside money for a rainy-day will endure it with less stress and long-term damage.

Personal Observances:

_____
_____
_____

October 19

Example

Inspiration: 2 Thessalonians 3:7 - For you yourselves know how you ought to follow our **example**. We were not idle when we were with you,

National Day: National Seafood Bisque Day

Anniversary: 1781 – British surrender at Yorktown ensuring American victory and Independence

Born Today: 1899 – Hal B. Wallis – movie producer

Motivation: "Example is not the main thing in influencing others. It is the only thing." – Albert Schweitzer

Battle's Bullet: If we study it, history is full of examples of virtually every experience we will encounter.

Personal Observances:
_____
_____
_____

October 20

Grow

Inspiration: **Ephesians 4:16** - From him the whole body, joined and held together by every supporting ligament, **grow**s and builds itself up in love, as each part does its work.

National Day: National Youth Confidence Day

Anniversary: 1944 – U.S. forces return to Philippines fulfilling General Douglas McArthur's "I Shall Return" promise

Born Today: 1931 – Mickey Mantle – baseball

Motivation: "You will either step forward into growth, or step backward into safety." – Abraham Maslow

Battle's Bullet: Anyone can destroy a creation. Only a creator can build or rebuild it.

Personal Observances:
_____
_____
_____

October 21

Overcomer

Inspiration: 1 John 5:4 - for everyone born of God **overcomes** the world. This is the victory that has **overcome** the world, even our faith.

National Day: National Reptile Awareness Day

Anniversary: 1744 – First use of word "Liberty" on flag in Massachusetts in defiance of England

Born Today: 1950 – Ronald McNair – physicist and astronaut

Motivation: "The greater the obstacle, the more glory in overcoming it." – Moliere

Battle's Bullet: Our parents and grandparents prioritized need over luxury and endured deprivation and sacrifice to gift us a land of plenty and leisure.

Personal Observances:

___
___
___

October  22

Patience

Inspiration: 2 Peter 3:9 - The Lord is not slow in keeping his promise, as some understand slowness. Instead he is **patient** with you, not wanting anyone to perish, but everyone to come to repentance.

National Day: National Make a Dog's Day

Anniversary: 1879 – Thomas Edison perfects carbon filament light bulb

Born Today: 1905 – Karl Jansky – engineer/radio astronomy

Motivation: "Patience is the key which solves all problems." --Sudanese proverb

Battle's Bullet: What we do today, tomorrow, and the rest of our tomorrow's is more important than what we did yesterday.

Personal Observances:
_____
_____
_____

October  23

Peace

Inspiration: Isaiah 32:17 - The fruit of that righteousness will be **peace**; its effect will be quietness and confidence forever.

National Day: Swallows Depart from San Juan Capistrano Day

Anniversary: 1941 – Disney movie *Dumbo* premieres

Born Today: 1925 – Johnny Carson – television

Motivation: "Let me bring peace into moments of chaos." – Jonathan Lochwood Huie

Battle's Bullet: Pressure makes us look for a quick and easy way out to resume a comfortable and peaceful course in life. "The easy way out" is seldom easy and less frequently the way out of any challenge.

Personal Observances:
___
___
___

October  24

Stand Firm

Inspiration:	2 Thessalonians 2:15 - So then, brothers and sisters, **stand firm** and hold fast to the teachings we passed on to you, whether by word of mouth or by letter.
National Day:	National Food Day
Anniversary:	1929 – Black Thursday stock market crash.
Born Today:	1932 – Stephen Covey – business/author – *7 Habits of Highly Effective People*
Motivation:	"Hold fast to what you already know and stand strong." – Jeffrey R. Holland
Battle's Bullet:	What kind of shoulders will we provide to those who come behind us on which to stand? I hope we don't let them down.

Personal Observances:
_____
_____
_____

October 25

Wisdom

Inspiration: **Proverbs 11:2** - When pride comes, then comes disgrace, but with humility comes **wisdom**.

National Day: Sourest Day

Anniversary: 1955 – First microwave oven sold by Tappan

Born Today: 1888 – Richard E. Byrd - explorer

Motivation: "He who seeks wisdom is a wise man; he who thinks he has found it is mad." Seneca the Younger

Battle's Bullet: We must make young people aware the wisdom of the ages is available for them from their parents and grandparents' generation.

Personal Observances:
_____
_____
_____

October  26

Perseverance

Inspiration:	2 Peter 1: 5-7 - For this very reason, make every effort to add to your faith goodness; and to goodness, knowledge; and to knowledge, self-control; and to self-control, **perseverance**; and to **perseverance**, godliness; and to godliness, mutual affection; and to mutual affection, love.
National Day:	National Day of the Deployed
Anniversary:	1787 – Federalist papers in support of the U.S. Constitution are published
Born Today:	1911 – Mahalia Jackson - music
Motivation:	"Don't let what you cannot do interfere with what you can do." – John Wooden
Battle's Bullet:	The easy way out is an oxymoron.

Personal Observances:

_____
_____
_____

October 27

Trustworthy - Trust

Inspiration: **Psalm 145:13** - Your kingdom is an everlasting kingdom, and your dominion endures through all generations. The Lord is **trustworthy** in all he promises and faithful in all he does.

National Day: National American Beer Day

Anniversary: 1775 – Continental Navy founded, which became the U.S. Navy

Born Today: 1858 – President Theodore Roosevelt (26)

Motivation: "God is faithful and He will take care of you if you trust Him." – BibleGodquotes.com

Battle's Bullet: The quality of our service always matters.

Personal Observances:

_____
_____
_____

October 28

Truth

Inspiration:	John 8:32 - Then you will know the **truth**, and the **truth** will set you free."
National Day:	National Chocolate Day
Anniversary:	1886 – Statue of Liberty is dedicated by President Grover Cleveland
Born Today:	1955 – Bill Gates – software leader
Motivation:	"If you tell the truth, you don't have to remember anything." – Mark Twain
Battle's Bullet:	Sometimes a person will only tell us part of the truth. They leave out other information that changes the entire meaning of the statement to obtain what they desire. Learning to listen with discernment is essential.

Personal Observances:
_____
_____
_____

October  29

Victorious

Inspiration: **Revelation 3:12** - The one who is **victorious** I will make a pillar in the temple of my God. Never again will they leave it. I will write on them the name of my God and the name of the city of my God, the new Jerusalem, which is coming down out of heaven from my God; and I will also write on them my new name.

National Day: National Cat Day

Anniversary: 1692 – Salem witch trials closed

Born Today: 1921 – Bill Mauldin - cartoonist

Motivation: "There is no victory without a battle." – Christine Caine

Battle's Bullet: Play till they rip your uniform off.

Personal Observances:
___
___
___

October 30

Thankful

Inspiration: **Colossians 3:15** - Let the peace of Christ rule in your hearts, since as members of one body you were called to peace. And be **thankful**.

National Day: National Speak Up for Service Day

Anniversary: 1873 – P. T. Barnum's circus premieres

Born Today: 1735 – President John Adams (2)

Motivation: "Gratitude teaches us to appreciate the rainbow and the storm." – Christina G. Hibbert, Psy.D.

Battle's Bullet: We don't have to receive a thank you to realize we impacted others.

Personal Observances:
_____
_____
_____

OCTOBER 31

Good Cheer

Inspiration: Mark 10:49 - Jesus stopped and said, "Call him." So they called to the blind man, "**Cheer** up! On your feet! He's calling you."

National Day: National Magic Day

Anniversary: 1950 – Earle Lloyd is the first African-American to play in an NBA game

Annual-Halloween.

Born Today: 1860 – Juliette Gordon Low – founder of Girl Scouts of America

Motivation: "Be of good cheer. The future is as bright as your faith."--Thomas S. Monson

Battle's Bullet: Life is a gift. We should value every moment.

Personal Observances:
___
___
___

NOVEMBER

November 1

Joy

Inspiration:	**John 16:22** - So with you: Now is your time of grief, but I will see you again and you will rejoice, and no one will take away your **joy**.
National Day:	National Family Literacy Day
Anniversary:	1800 – President John Adams is the first resident of The White House
Born Today:	1880 – Grantland Rice - writer
Motivation:	"Joy is not in things; it is in us." – Richard Wagner
Battle's Bullet:	Enjoy every stage of life while you can.

Personal Observances:

_____
_____
_____

November 2

Honor

Inspiration: John 5:23 - that all may **honor** the Son just as they **honor** the Father. Whoever does not **honor** the Son does not **honor** the Father, who sent him.

National Day: National Deviled Egg Day

Anniversary: 1824 – Andrew Jackson elected president

Born Today: 1795 – President James Polk (11)
1865 – President Warren Harding (29)

Motivation: "He who lives without discipline, dies without honor." --Icelandic proverb

Battle's Bullet: Always be on time! Tardiness is disrespectful of others.

Personal Observances:
_____
_____
_____

November 3

Heart

Inspiration: 1 Samuel 12:24 - But be sure to fear the Lord and serve him faithfully with all your **heart**; consider what great things he has done for you.

National Day: National Housewife's Day

Anniversary: 1952 – Clarence Birdseye first markets frozen peas

Born Today: 1793 – Stephen F. Austin – founder of Texas

Motivation: "If you don't think you have any blessings remember your heart is still beating." – Worshipgifs

Battle's Bullet: I strive to touch the individuals I encounter in a way that will positively influence them and their families beyond the present as well.

Personal Observances:
_____
_____
_____

November 4

Hope

Inspiration:	**Lamentations 3:25** -The Lord is good to those whose **hope** is in him, to the one who seeks him;
National Day:	National Candy Day
Anniversary:	1646 – Massachusetts employs death penalty for denial Holy Bible is God's word
Born Today:	1879 – Will Rogers - Humorist
Motivation:	"Hope is seeing light in spite of being surrounded by darkness." – Live Purposefully Now
Battle's Bullet:	I hope that everyone arrives at a point in their journey to consider how they might impact our future descendants and the world they will inhabit.

Personal Observances:

_____
_____
_____

NOVEMBER 5

Courage

Inspiration: **Ezra 10:4** - Rise up; this matter is in your hands. We will support you, so take **courage** and do it."

National Day: National Love Your Red Hair Day

Anniversary: 1895 – George Selden issued first patent for a gasoline powered car

Born Today: 1885 – Will Durant - author

Motivation: "Always remember your present situation is not your final destination. The best is yet to come." – Live Purposely Now

Battle's Bullet: None of us can do everything in public service, but we should all do at least one more thing as citizens, so we don't become subjects.

Personal Observances:
___
___
___

November 6

Act

Inspiration: **Colossians 4:5** - Be wise in the way you **act** toward outsiders; make the most of every opportunity.

National Day: National Nachos Day

Anniversary: 1869 – First College football game – Rutgers 6, Princeton 4

Born Today: 1861 – James Naismith – invented basketball

Motivation: "Be content to act and leave the talking to others." --Baltasar Gracian

Battle's Bullet: No cure or growth comes from living in past actions.

Personal Observances:
_____
_____
_____

NOVEMBER 7

Fearless

Inspiration: **Psalm 55:19** - God, who is enthroned from of old, who does **not** change— he will hear them and humble them, because they have no **fear** of God.

National Day: National Bittersweet Chocolate with Almonds Day

Anniversary: 1876 – Disputed presidential election between Hayes and Tilden. Not resolved until March 3, 1877 (115 days later).

Born Today: 1918 – Billy Graham - evangelist

Motivation: "Do not fear failure but rather fear not trying." – Roy T. Bennett

Battle's Bullet: Many things we fear most never occur.

Personal Observances:
_____
_____
_____

November 8

Humble

Inspiration: Isaiah 26:5 - He **humble**s those who dwell on high, he lays the lofty city low; he levels it to the ground and casts it down to the dust.

National Day: National Parents as Teachers' Day

Anniversary: 1731 – Benjamin Franklin opens the first library in the colonies in Philadelphia

Born Today: 1900 – Margaret Mitchell - author

Motivation: "Be modest, humble, simple. Control your anger." --Abraham Cahan

Battle's Bullet: To be an effective leader, we must also be a good follower.

Personal Observances:
_____
_____
_____

November 9

Faith - Faithful

Inspiration:	**Hebrews 12:2** - fixing our eyes on Jesus, the pioneer and perfecter of **faith**. For the joy set before him he endured the cross, scorning its shame, and sat down at the right hand of the throne of God.
National Day:	National Scrapple Day
Anniversary:	1620 – Mayflower first spots land of Cape Cod
Born Today:	1914 – Hedy Lamarr – invented wireless technology
Motivation:	"Faith is all about believing, you don't know how it will happen, but you know it will." – love&inspiration.com
Battle's Bullet:	If we remain true to our principles and values, our route will be smoother, and we will travel farther toward our desired destination than if we are less faithful in our discipline.

Personal Observances:

_____
_____
_____

November 10

Provision

Inspiration: **Psalm 111:9** - He **provided** redemption for his people; he ordained his covenant forever— holy and awesome is his name.

National Day: Marine Corps Birthday

Anniversary: 1954 – Marine Corps memorial dedicated in Arlington, Virginia

Born Today: 1939 – Russell Means – Ogalala Sioux activist

Motivation: "Lord, give me firmness without hardness, steadfastness without dogmatism, love without weakness." ~ Jim Elliot

Battle's Bullet: Worry is an exercise that burns calories but provides negative results instead of positive ones.

Personal Observances:
___
___
___

November 11

Mercy

Inspiration: **Psalm 116:1** - I love the Lord, for he heard my voice; he heard my cry for **mercy**.

National Day: National Sundae Day

Anniversary: 1918 – Armistice ending World War I goes into effect at 11:00 a.m.

Born Today: 1885 – George S. Patton - military

Motivation: "Mercy did not exist in the primordial life. It was misunderstood for fear, and such misunderstandings made for death." - Jack London

Battle's Bullet: When we turn the responsibility of outcomes over to Him, we can trust that He will take better care of us than we can take care of ourselves.

Personal Observances:
_____
_____
_____

November 12

Forgiveness

Inspiration: Acts 13:38 - "Therefore, my friends, I want you to know that through Jesus the **forgiveness** of sins is proclaimed to you.

National Day: National Chicken Soup for the Soul Day

Anniversary: 1880 – *Ben-Hur: A Tale of the Christ* is published by author, Lew Wallace

Born Today: 1815 – Elizabeth Cady Stanton, Women's Rights advocate

Motivation: "If we really want to love, we must learn how to forgive." – Mother Teresa

Battle's Bullet: Focusing on the present instead of worrying about the past provides us peace, and we will be more successful.

Personal Observances:
_____
_____
_____

November  13

Grace

Inspiration: 1 Peter 1:13 - Therefore, with minds that are alert and fully sober, set your hope on the **grace** to be brought to you when Jesus Christ is revealed at his coming.

National Day: National Indian Pudding Day

Anniversary: 1865 – U.S. issues the first "gold certificates"

Born Today: 1911 – Buck O'Neil - baseball

Motivation: "Fortunately, God doesn't keep score the way we humans do. (If he did, there wouldn't be one of us still standing.)" – Dr. Tim Kimmel and Darcy Kimmel

Battle's Bullet: Each of us is blessed with unique gifts and talents, enabling us to positively impact the coming world.

Personal Observances:
___
___
___

November 14

Love

Inspiration: Jude 1:21 - keep yourselves in God's **love** as you wait for the mercy of our Lord Jesus Christ to bring you to eternal life.

National Day: National Family PJ Day

Anniversary: 1851 – *Moby Dick* by Herman Melville is first published

Born Today: 1765 – Robert Fulton - inventor

Motivation: "God teaches us to love by putting some unlovely people around us." – Rick Warren

Battle's Bullet: I love humor and often see it during the toughest of times. It serves me to defuse tension.

Personal Observances:
_____
_____
_____

November 15

Rejoice

Inspiration: **1 Corinthians 13:6** - Love does not delight in evil but **rejoice**s with the truth.

National Day: National Philanthropy Day

Anniversary: 1777 – Articles of Confederation approved by The Continental Congress as the first constitution of The United States

Born Today: 1887 – Georgia O'Keeffe - painter

Motivation: "Brave men rejoice in adversity. Just as brave soldiers triumph in war." – Lucius Annaeus Seneca

Battle's Bullet: We are blessed to enjoy things our parents could only dream about, and our grandparents couldn't conceive.

Personal Observances:
_____
_____
_____

November 16

Adversity – Trials - Obstacles

Inspiration: **2 Thessalonians 1:4** - Therefore, among God's churches we boast about your perseverance and faith in all the persecutions and **trials** you are enduring.

National Day: National Fast-Food Day

Anniversary: 1798 – Kentucky is the first state to nullify an act of Congress

Born Today: 1873 – W. C. Handy – blues music innovator

Motivation: "One's best success comes after their greatest disappointments." – Henry Ward Beecher

Battle's Bullet: We all have challenges and trials, and no one wants to hear someone feel sorry for himself.

Personal Observances:
_____
_____
_____

November 17

Encouragement

Inspiration: **Romans 15:4** - For everything that was written in the past was written to teach us, so that through the endurance taught in the Scriptures and the **encouragement** they provide we might have hope.

National Day: National Take a Hike Day

Anniversary: 1913 – First ship sails through U.S. constructed Panama Canal

Born Today: 1916 – Shelby Foote - historian

Motivation: "God sometimes takes us into troubled waters not to drown us but to cleanse us." – geckoandfly.com

Battle's Bullet: Whether we emerge from this or a future wilderness soon, or if it takes a long time, what can we do each day to survive, thrive, and encourage our family and friends?

Personal Observances:
___
___
___

November 18

Endurance

Inspiration: Revelation 13:10 - "If anyone is to go into captivity, into captivity they will go. If anyone is to be killed with the sword, with the sword they will be killed." This calls for patient **endurance** and faithfulness on the part of God's people.

National Day: Mickey Mouse's Birthday

Anniversary: 1928 – *Steamboat Willie*, first Mickey Mouse cartoon released

Born Today: 1923 – Alan Shepard - astronaut

Motivation: "Scars are not a weakness, they are a sign of survival and endurance." – Rodney A. Winters

Battle's Bullet: There is no rainbow without the rain, and we don't develop endurance without sacrificing strength through the exercise that pushes us beyond our comfort level.

Personal Observances:
_____
_____
_____

November 19

Example

Inspiration: **1 Corinthians 10:11** - These things happened to them as **example**s and were written down as warnings for us, on whom the culmination of the ages has come.

National Day: National Play Monopoly Day

Anniversary: 1863 – President Abraham Lincoln delivers the Gettysburg address

Born Today: 1831 – President James A. Garfield (20)

Motivation: "You can teach better with your example than by your words." – Reed Markham

Battle's Bullet: We are wise to search the examples of those who overcame significant challenges and setbacks to recover more quickly and soar higher after their misfortunes.

Personal Observances:
_____
_____
_____

November 20

Grow

Inspiration:	**Job 17:9** - Nevertheless, the righteous will hold to their ways, and those with clean hands will **grow** stronger.
National Day:	National Child's Day
Anniversary:	1789 – New Jersey is the first state to ratify *The Bill of Rights*
Born Today:	1889 – Edwin Hubble - astronomer
Motivation:	"If you don't get uncomfortable leaving your comfort zone, then you haven't really left it." – Tim Brownson
Battle's Bullet:	The more I know, the less I know, and that's all I know.

Personal Observances:

_____
_____
_____

November 21

Overcomer

Inspiration: Matthew 16:18 - And I tell you that you are Peter, and on this rock I will build my church, and the gates of Hades will not **overcome** it.

National Day: National Gingerbread Cookie Day

Anniversary: 1620 – Pilgrims sign the Mayflower Compact at Cape Cod

Born Today: 1834 – Henrietta "Hetty" Green – business and finance

Motivation: "Your hardest times often lead to the greatest moments of your life. Keep going. Tough situations build strong people in the end." – Roy T. Bennett

Battle's Bullet: We should be Lone Ranger's to help others overcome their challenges.

Personal Observances:
_____
_____
_____

November  22

Patience

Inspiration:	**Psalm 89:2** - I will declare that your love **stand**s **firm** forever, that you have established your faithfulness in heaven itself.
National Day:	National Cranberry Relish Day
Anniversary:	1963 – President John F. Kennedy is assassinated
Born Today:	1942 – Guion Bluford - astronaut
Motivation:	"Some of your greatest blessings come with patience." – Warren Wiersbe
Battle's Bullet:	Most rich and successful people paid their dues. We should learn from them, but not envy them.

Personal Observances:
___
___
___

NOVEMBER 23

Peace

Inspiration: **2 Timothy 2:22** - Flee the evil desires of youth and pursue righteousness, faith, love and **peace**, along with those who call on the Lord out of a pure heart.

National Day: National Espresso Day

Anniversary: 1945 – United States ends most World War II food rationing

Born Today: 1804 – President Franklin Pierce (14)

Motivation: "When the power of love overcomes the love of power the world will know peace." – Jimi Hendrix

Battle's Bullet: People of faith believe the object of their faith will deliver peace to them.

Personal Observances:
_____
_____
_____

November 24

Stand Firm

Inspiration:	**Ephesians 6:14 - Stand firm** then, with the belt of truth buckled around your waist, with the breastplate of righteousness in place,
National Day:	National Sardines Day
Anniversary:	1874 – Joseph Glidden patents barbed wire
Born Today:	1784 – President Zachary Taylor (12)
Motivation:	"Not gold, but only man can make a people great and strong; men who, for truth and honor's sake, stand fast and suffer long." - Ralph Waldo Emerson
Battle's Bullet:	Too often, people insist upon their rights, but fewer stand tall, carrying their share of their duty as citizens.

Personal Observances:
___
___
___

November 25

Wisdom

Inspiration:	**Psalm 111:10 - The fear of the Lord is the beginning of** wisdom; all who follow his precepts have good understanding. To him belongs eternal praise.
National Day:	Thanksgiving 4th Thursday
Anniversary:	1792 – *The Farmer's Almanac* is first published by Benjamin Banneker
Born Today:	1835 – Andrew Carnegie – industrialist and philanthropist
Motivation:	"Knowledge is knowing what to say. Wisdom is knowing whether or not to say it." – Unknown
Battle's Bullet:	Revere the past. The wisdom of the ages is at our fingertips.

Personal Observances:

_____
_____
_____

November 26

Perseverance

Inspiration: **Revelation 2:2** - I know your deeds, your hard work and your **perseverance**. I know that you cannot tolerate wicked people, that you have tested those who claim to be apostles but are not, and have found them false.

National Day: National Cake Day

Anniversary: 1789 – First national Thanksgiving is celebrated in America

Born Today: 1922 – Charles Schulz – cartoonist famous for *Peanuts*

Motivation: "The difference between a successful person and others is not a lack of strength, not a lack of knowledge, but rather a lack in will." - Vince Lombardi Jr.

Battle's Bullet: Maintain a structure for your days and the discipline to persevere each day.

Personal Observances:
_____
_____
_____

NOVEMBER 27

Trustworthy - Trust

Inspiration: **Psalm 56:3-4** - When I am afraid, I put my **trust** in you. In God, whose word I praise— in God I **trust** and am not afraid. What can mere mortals do to me?

National Day: National Craft Jerky Day

Anniversary: 1920 – First U.S. super hero film, *The Mask of Zorro*, premieres in New York

Born Today: 1853 – Bat Masterson - lawman

Motivation: "Respect is earned. Honesty is appreciated. Trust is gained. Loyalty is appreciated." – Unknown

Battle's Bullet: We inherited our distrust of government at all levels from our forefathers. Their lives validated the experience the founders used in establishing our country.

Personal Observances:
___
___
___

November  28

Truth

Inspiration: 3 John 8 - We ought therefore to show hospitality to such people so that we may work together for the **truth**.

National Day: National French Toast Day

Anniversary: 1895 – First car race in U.S. from Chicago to Evanston, Illinois

Born Today: 1929 – Berry Gordy Jr. - music

Motivation: "It's not about who is real to your face. It's about who stays real behind your back." – Unknown

Battle's Bullet: It is common for us to accept what people tell us because we want to believe everyone is truthful.

Personal Observances:
_____
_____
_____

NOVEMBER 29

Victorious

Inspiration: **Revelation 15:2** - And I saw what looked like a sea of glass glowing with fire and, standing beside the sea, those who had been **victorious** over the beast and its image and over the number of its name. They held harps given them by God

National Day: Electronic Greetings Day

Anniversary: 1877 – Thomas Edison first demonstrates the phonograph

Born Today: 1832 – Louisa May Alcott - author

Motivation: "We will be victorious if we have not forgotten how to learn." – Rosa Luxemburg

Battle's Bullet: Navigating change to success requires: Anticipating change, recognizing it as early as possible, and Adapting to it as quickly as possible.

Personal Observances:

_____
_____
_____

November  30

Thankful

Inspiration: **Ephesians 5:20** - always giving **thanks** to God the Father for everything, in the name of our Lord Jesus Christ.

National Day: Computer Security Day

Anniversary: 1866 – First underwater highway tunnel construction begins in Chicago

Born Today: 1835 – Mark Twain – humorist/author

Motivation: "I'm thankful for nights that turned into mornings, friends that turned into family, and dreams that turned into reality." – quotesideas.com

Battle's Bullet: There is ALWAYS an alternative choice.

Personal Observances:
_____
_____
_____

DECEMBER

December 1

Joy

Inspiration: Luke 1:14 - He will be a **joy** and delight to you, and many will rejoice because of his birth,

National Day: Rosa Parks Day

Anniversary: 1824 – U.S. House of Representatives begins presidential election deliberations

Born Today: 1913 – Mary Martin – actress (Peter Pan)

Motivation: "Christian joy is letting Christ live His life out through you so that what He is, you become." – David Jeremiah

Battle's Bullet: Relax and enjoy your safe harbor upon completion of your mission. Know your broadened shoulders, and the seed you planted will grow in the future and benefit others.

Personal Observances:

December 2

Honor

Inspiration: **1 Corinthians 6:20** - you were bought at a price. Therefore **honor** God with your bodies.

National Day: Special Education Day

Anniversary: 1823 – President James Monroe issues The Monroe Doctrine

Born Today: 1928 – Dan Jenkins - author

Motivation: "I would prefer even to fail with honor than win by cheating." – Sophocles

Battle's Bullet: Principle over power. Honor over ambition.

Personal Observances:

_____
_____
_____

DECEMBER 3

Heart

Inspiration: John 14:1 - "Do not let your **heart**s be troubled. You believe in God; believe also in me."

National Day: National Roof Over Your Head Day

Anniversary: 1847 – Frederick Douglass first publishes his newspaper, *The North Star*

Born Today: 1755 – Gilbert Stuart - painter

Motivation: "Allow God to continually soften your heart so that it beats for what His heart beats for – People." – Christine Caine

Battle's Bullet: Regardless of our achievements or the gifts that we provide others, the summit is ever elusive until our life on this earth is over.

Personal Observances:
_____
_____
_____

December 4

Hope

Inspiration: Micah 7:7 - But as for me, I watch in **hope** for the Lord, I wait for God my Savior; my God will hear me.

National Day: National Cookie Day

Anniversary: 1843 – Manila paper is patented in Massachusetts

Born Today: 1912 – Greg "Pappy" Boyington – Pilot (Medal of Honor)

Motivation: "Never talk defeat. Use words like hope, belief, faith, victory." – Norman Vincent Peale

Battle's Bullet: Only an object that is unchangeable and eternal is trustworthy of our Hope.

Personal Observances:
_____
_____
_____

December 5

Courage

Inspiration:	**Matthew 14:27** - But Jesus immediately said to them: "Take **courage**! It is I. Don't be afraid."
National Day:	Bathtub Party Day
Anniversary:	1492 – Christopher Columbus discovers Hispaniola
Born Today:	1782 – President Martin Van Buren (8)
	1901 – Walt Disney - entertainment
Motivation:	"Uncertainty is the essence of life and it fuels opportunity." – Tina Seelig
Battle's Bullet:	I will, is no substitute for I DID.

Personal Observances:
___
___
___

December 6

Act

Inspiration:	**James 2:17** - In the same way, faith by itself, if it is not accompanied by **act**ion, is dead.
National Day:	St. Nicholas Day
Anniversary:	1865 – 13th Amendment to Constitution ratified eliminating slavery
Born Today:	1898 – Alfred Eisenstaedt - photographer
Motivation:	"Believe and act as if it were impossible to fail." – Charles F. Kettering
Battle's Bullet:	Be creative. Always be thinking of ways to improve yourself and the things you're doing.

Personal Observances:
_____
_____
_____

December 7

Fearless

Inspiration: **Isaiah 41:10** - So do **not fear**, for I am with you; do not be dismayed, for I am your God. I will strengthen you and help you; I will uphold you with my righteous right hand.

National Day: National Pearl Harbor Remembrance Day

Anniversary: 1941 – Pearl Harbor is attacked without warning by Japan catapulting the U.S. into World War II

Born Today: 1863 – Richard W. Sears – business (Sears, Roebuck & Co.)

Motivation: "Once you become fearless, life becomes limitless." – Unknown

Battle's Bullet: I will never quit attempting to be a better person and example every day.

Personal Observances:
___
___
___

December 8

Humble

Inspiration: **Philippians 2:8** - And being found in appearance as a man, he **humble**d himself by becoming obedient to death— even death on a cross!

National Day: National Brownie Day

Anniversary: 1941 – President Franklin Roosevelt delivers "Day of Infamy" speech to U.S. Congress

Born Today: 1765 – Eli Whitney – inventor (mass production)

Motivation: "Work hard in silence. Let success make the noise." – Unknown

Battle's Bullet: I hope you benefit from my communications half as much as your positive comments encourage me.

Personal Observances:
___
___
___

December  9

Faith - Faithful

Inspiration: Matthew 25:21 - "His master replied, 'Well done, good and **faith**ful servant! You have been **faith**ful with a few things; I will put you in charge of many things. Come and share your master's happiness!'

National Day: National Pastry Day

Anniversary: 1965 – *A Charlie Brown Christmas* premieres on CBS television

Born Today: 1906 – Grace Hopper – U.S Navy and mathematician

Motivation: "Faith in God includes faith in His timing." – Neal A. Maxwell

Battle's Bullet: If we are faithful to pursue and persist in attempting to accomplish our destiny, we will finish our journey in a safe harbor.

Personal Observances:
___
___
___

December  10

Provision

Inspiration:	**Titus 3:14** - Our people must learn to devote themselves to doing what is good, in order to **provide** for urgent needs and not live unproductive lives.
National Day:	National Rights Day
Anniversary:	1906 – President Theodore Roosevelt is the first American awarded the Nobel Peace Prize
Born Today:	1787 – Thomas Hopkins Gallaudet - educator
Motivation:	"You can be overlooked and undervalued, but you are not forgotten." – John Gray
Battle's Bullet:	We are blessed to live in a country that provides us the liberty to live in the "pursuit of happiness" we define and desire at the pace we decide to travel.

Personal Observances:
___
___
___

December 11

Mercy

Inspiration: Psalm 27:7 - Hear my voice when I call, LORD; be **merciful** to me and answer me.

National Day: National App Day

Anniversary: 1909 – Moving pictures in color demonstrated in New York

Born Today: 1830 – Kamehameha V – King of Hawaii

Motivation: "Fight the good fight of faith, and God will give you spiritual mercies." - George Whitefield

Battle's Bullet: Don't let troubles biting your ankles drop your view from the future to only the present problem.

Personal Observances:
___
___
___

December 12

Forgiveness

Inspiration: **Ephesians** 1:7 - In him we have redemption through his blood, the **forgive**ness of sins, in accordance with the riches of God's grace

National Day: National Ding-A-Ling Day

Anniversary: 1917 – Boys Town formed in Omaha, Nebraska by Father Flanagan

Born Today: 1915 – Frank Sinatra - entertainer

Motivation: "I forgive myself and set myself free." – Louise Hay

Battle's Bullet: There is no such thing as a dumb question, just dumb answers.

Personal Observances:
_____
_____
_____

December  13

Grace

Inspiration: Titus 2:11 - For the **grace** of God has appeared that offers salvation to all people.

National Day: National Guard Birthday

Anniversary: 1759 – The first music store in U.S. opens in Philadelphia

Born Today: 1887 – Sgt. Alvin York – World War I Medal of Honor recipient

Motivation: "Grace is opposed to earning, but not to effort." – Dallas Willard

Battle's Bullet: When we lift others with our encouraging words, there is no limit to the impact of the gift to future generations as it ripples across time.

Personal Observances:
_____
_____
_____

December  14

Love

Inspiration:	Mark 12:31 - The second is this: '**Love** your neighbor as yourself.' There is no commandment greater than these."
National Day:	Monkey Day
Anniversary:	1774 – New Hampshire militia attack Fort William & Mary in first skirmish of the American Revolution
Born Today:	1896 – Jimmy Doolittle – aviator/World War II hero
Motivation:	"Love is a gift of God." – Jack Hyles
Battle's Bullet:	Man loves to be in control, but we should emphasize God's faithful promises to us.

Personal Observances:

___
___
___

December 15

Rejoice

Inspiration: **Joel 2:12** - "Even now," declares the Lord, "return to me with all your **heart**, with fasting and weeping and mourning."

National Day: Bill of Rights Day

Anniversary: 1791 – Bill of Rights ratified

Born Today: 1892 – J. Paul Getty - industrialist

Motivation: "What is, is simply what it is. Allow it and rejoice in it." – Deepak Chopra

Battle's Bullet: Positive people face adversity with the perspective that it will usually be a relatively short-term situation and that lessons can benefit them for the remainder of their life.

Personal Observances:
___
___
___

December  16

Adversity – Trials - Obstacles

Inspiration: **Revelation 3:10** - Since you have kept my command to endure patiently, I will also keep you from the hour of **trial** that is going to come on the whole world to test the inhabitants of the earth.

National Day: National Chocolate Covered Anything Day

Anniversary: 1773 – Boston Tea Party as the Sons of Liberty protest by throwing tea into harbor

Born Today: 1928 – Philip K. Dick - author

Motivation: "The flower that blooms in adversity is the rarest and most beautiful of all." – Walt Disney

Battle's Bullet: Beware of the unintended consequences of your actions.

Personal Observances:
___
___
___

December 17

Encouragement

Inspiration: **Titus 1:9** - He must hold firmly to the trustworthy message as it has been taught, so that he can **encourage** others by sound doctrine and refute those who oppose it.

National Day: Wright Brothers Day

Anniversary: 1903 – Wright Brothers successfully fly first power-controlled airplane at Kitty Hawk, North Carolina

Born Today: 1894 – Arthur Fiedler - music

Motivation: "Your mind will always believe everything you tell it. Feed it faith. Feed it truth. Feed it with love." – dailyfunnyquote.com

Battle's Bullet: I encourage you always give your best effort. Don't let others' habits deter you from focusing your energy on accomplishing your goal or dream.

Personal Observances:
___
___
___

December 18

Endurance

Inspiration:	**Revelation 14:12** - This calls for patient **endurance** on the part of the people of God who keep his commands and remain faithful to Jesus.
National Day:	National Twin Day
Anniversary:	1917 – 18th amendment to the Constitution is passed prohibiting alcohol sales and sent to the states for ratification
Born Today:	1946 – Steven Spielberg - entertainment
Motivation:	"The amount of endurance you develop is determined by the amount of stress you are willing to overcome." – Michael D'Aulerio
Battle's Bullet:	Our parents and grandparents, who endured the great depression and World War II, couldn't imagine the grandeur so frequently taken for granted in the current generation.

Personal Observances:

_____
_____
_____

DECEMBER 19

Example

Inspiration:	**Hebrews 4:11** - Let us, therefore, make every effort to enter that rest, so that no one will perish by following their **example** of disobedience.
National Day:	National Hard Candy Day
Anniversary:	1732 – Benjamin Franklin begins publication of *Poor Richard's Almanack*
Born Today:	1875 – Carter G. Woodson – historian
Motivation:	"A leader leads by example not force." – Sun Tzu
Battle's Bullet:	How we do something often has more impact than what we do.

Personal Observances:

_____
_____
_____

December 20

Grow

Inspiration:	**Revelation 2:3** - You have persevered and have endured hardships for my name, and have not **grow**n weary.
National Day:	National Sangria Day
Anniversary:	1919 – U. S. House of Representatives restricts immigration
Born Today:	1868 – Harvey Firestone - industrialist
Motivation:	"Personal development is the belief you are worth the effort, time, and energy needed to develop yourself." – Denis Waitley
Battle's Bullet:	To realize personal growth, prosper long term, and lead others, it is imperative to resist the temptation to fall into "groupthink."

Personal Observances:

_____
_____
_____

December 21

Overcomer

Inspiration: **1 John 5:5** - Who is it that **overcome**s the world? Only the one who believes that Jesus is the Son of God.

National Day: Crossword Puzzle Day

Anniversary: 1891 – First game of basketball based on James Naismith's rules is played in Massachusetts

Born Today: 1603 – Roger Williams – founder of Providence Plantation, Rhode Island

Motivation: "Don't let your struggle become your identity." – buttergirldiaries.com

Battle's Bullet: I hope the wind and sun are at your back when you next find yourself in rough waters, and your previous experiences will serve you to overcome each turbulence in the successful navigation of your journey.

Personal Observances:
_____
_____
_____

December 22

Patience

Inspiration: 2 Peter 3:15 - Bear in mind that our Lord's **patience** means salvation, just as our dear brother Paul also wrote you with the wisdom that God gave him.

National Day: National Date Nut Bread Day

Anniversary: 1883 – Thomas Edison creates the first string of Christmas lights

Born Today: 1912 – Lady Bird Johnson – First Lady

Motivation: "The lessons we learn from patience will cultivate our character, lift our lives, and heighten our happiness." – Dieter F. Uchtdorf

Battle's Bullet: It's never too late to choose the right path for our life. If it comes late, don't miss it.

Personal Observances:
___
___
___

December 23

Peace

Inspiration: Isaiah 9:7 - Of the greatness of his government and **peace** there will be no end. He will reign on David's throne and over his kingdom, establishing and upholding it with justice and righteousness from that time on and forever.

National Day: Festivus

Anniversary: 1919 – Alice H. Parker patents the gas heating furnace

Born Today: 1805 – Joseph Smith – Religious Leader

Motivation: "If it costs you your peace, it's too expensive." – quotling.com

Battle's Bullet: It is advantageous to grow older and more experienced because we have learned so many of the things, we worried about were not worth the negative energy expended worrying about them.

Personal Observances:
___
___
___

December 24

Stand Firm

Inspiration:	**James 5:8** - You too, be patient and **stand firm**, because the Lord's coming is near.
National Day:	National Eggnog Day
Anniversary:	1814 – Treaty of Ghent ends the War of 1812
Born Today:	1809 – Kit Carson – frontiersman/scout
	1905 – Howard Hughes – multi-faceted business magnate
Motivation:	"Stand fast and all temptation to transgress repel." – John Milton
Battle's Bullet:	We can be our own worst enemy when we stand in the door of an inevitable change and try to stop it.

Personal Observances:

_____
_____
_____

December 25

Wisdom

Inspiration: Isaiah 9:6 - For to us a child is born, to us a son is given, and the government will be on his shoulders. And he will be called Wonderful Counselor, Mighty God, Everlasting Father, Prince of Peace.

National Day: Christmas

Anniversary: Christmas

Born Today: Christ's birth celebrated
1821 – Clara Barton – Red Cross founder

Motivation: "Let go of things you can't change, focus on things you can." – funnywallpaper24

Battle's Bullet: Be careful how much government you desire. You may get it and more.

Personal Observances:
___
___
___

December 26

Perseverance

Inspiration:	**Revelation 2:19** - I know your deeds, your love and faith, your service and **perseverance**, and that you are now doing more than you did at first.
National Day:	National Thank You Note Day
Anniversary:	1776 – George Washington's troops defeat the Hessians in the Battle of Trenton after crossing the Delaware River Christmas night
Born Today:	1837 – George Dewey – U.S. Naval Commander
Motivation:	"Life is tough. You are tougher. Life is persistent. You are relentless." - @trainersarahalmand
Battle's Bullet:	**Aim High! Work Hard! NEVER Quit!**

Personal Observances:

_____
_____
_____

December 27

Trustworthy - Trust

Inspiration: **Psalm 37:3** - **Trust** in the Lord and do good; dwell in the land and enjoy safe pasture.

National Day: National Fruitcake Day

Anniversary: 1932 – Radio City Music Hall opens in New York City

Born Today: 1948 – Juan Felipe Herrera - poet

Motivation: "Trust only movement. Life happens at the level of events, not of words." – lifehacks.io

Battle's Bullet: Treat other people's property as you want others to treat yours and you will be trusted.

Personal Observances:
_____
_____
_____

December  28

Truth

Inspiration:	**Psalm 25:5** - Guide me in your **truth** and teach me, for you are God my Savior, and my hope is in you all day long.
National Day:	Pledge of Allegiance Day
Anniversary:	1902 – First indoor pro football game in Madison Square Garden in New York
Born Today:	1856 – President Woodrow Wilson (28)
Motivation:	"The naked truth is always better than the best dressed lie." – Unknown
Battle's Bullet:	Truth is the first casualty in debate when the quest for power prevails over principle.

Personal Observances:
___
___
___

December 29

Victorious

Inspiration: **Revelation 21:7** - Those who are **victorious** will inherit all this, and I will be their God and they will be my children.

National Day: National Pepper Pot Day

Anniversary: 1890 – Wounded Knee massacre

Born Today: 1808 – President Andrew Johnson (17)

Motivation: "Leaders aren't born they are made. And they are made like anything else through hard work. And that's the price we'll have to pay to achieve that goal, or any goal." – Vince Lombardi

Battle's Bullet: When we deliver excellence, we receive recognition for the superior level of service we provide, and doors of opportunity will open to us.

Personal Observances:

_____
_____
_____

December 30

Thankful

Inspiration:	**Hebrews 12:28** - Therefore, since we are receiving a kingdom that cannot be shaken, let us be **thankful**, and so worship God acceptably with reverence and awe
National Day:	Bacon Day
Anniversary:	1924 – Astronomer Edwin Hubble announces the existence of other galaxies
Born Today:	1975 – Tiger Woods - golf
Motivation:	"The thankful receiver bears a plentiful harvest." – William Blake
Battle's Bullet:	Thankfully, we all don't fail under pressure all of the time. Those successes under stress build our society and forge progress.

Personal Observances:
___
___
___

December  31

Good Cheer

Inspiration: **Revelation 22:20-21** – He who testifies to these things says, "Yes, I am coming soon." Amen. Come, Lord Jesus. The grace of the Lord Jesus be with God's people. Amen.

National Day: New Year's Eve

Anniversary: 1879 – Thomas Edison publicly demonstrates his incandescent light

Born Today: 1880 – George Marshall – General – Nobel Peace prize winner

Motivation: "Happiness is an attitude. We either make ourselves miserable, or happy and strong. The amount of work is the same." – Francesca Reigler

Battle's Bullet: Discouragement kills more enthusiasm, squanders incredible amounts of energy, and thwarts civilization's advancement by killing or delaying the development of many ideas.

Personal Observances:
___
___
___

Bibliography

Ambrose, Stephen E., *Undaunted Courage*, New York, Simon & Schuster, 1996.

www.arkinthedesert.com

Austin American Statesman, Austin, 1986.

Battle, Richard, *Conquering Life's Course: Common Sense in Chaotic Times*, Parker, Outskirts Press, 2019.

Battle, Richard, *Navigating Life's Journey: Common Sense in Uncommon Times*, Parker, Outskirts Press, 2020.

Battle, Richard, *Surviving Grief by God's Grace*, Bloomington, AuthorHouse, 2002.

Battle, Richard, *The Four-Letter Word that Builds Character*, Austin, Volunteer Concepts, 2006.

Battle, Richard, *The Master's Sales Secrets,* Parker, Outskirts Press, 2018.

Battle, Richard, *Unwelcome Opportunity: Overcoming Life's Greatest Challenges*, Parker, Outskirts Press 2018.

www.BibleGodquotes.com

Biography On-Line. www.biographyonline.net.

www.brainyquote.com.

www.buttergirldiaries.com

www.christianquotes.info.

www.crosscards.com

www.dailyfunnyquote.com

www.dandelionquotes.com

D'Sousa, Dinesh, Ronald Reagan: *How an Ordinary Man Became an Extraordinary Leader*, New York, *The Free Press*, 1997.

The Free Dictionary by Farlex on-line dictionary. http://www.thefreedictionary.com/.

www.funnyclub.com

www.funnywallpaper24.com

www.geckoandfly.com

www.gratitudehabitat.com

The Holy Bible, New International Version, www.biblegateway.com.

www.ibelieve.com

www.lifehacks.io

www.love&inspiration.com

Merriam-Webster on-line dictionary, www.merriam-webster.com.

www.mydearvalentine.com

National Day calendar, www.nationaldaycalendar.com.

www.onthisday.com.

www.picturequotes.com

www.positivelifetips.com

www.purehappylife.com

www.Quotecounterquote.com.

www.quotling.com

www.quotesideas.com

Semi-Tough movie, 1977

www.sevenly.org

www.therapy-talk.com

www.tightentheslack.com

www.wikipedia.org

Winning Path

www.wiseoldsayings.com

ABOUT THE AUTHOR
RICHARD V. BATTLE
MULTI AWARD-WINNING AUTHOR, SPEAKER AND ADVISOR

Richard is the multi award-winning author of seven previously published books.

He has been a public speaker and trainer for over 30 years on topics including, leadership, motivation, faith, sales, and volunteerism.

Richard was an executive with **KeyTrak** (a Reynolds and Reynolds company), and has more than 40 years of experience in sales, executive management and leadership in various business entities.

He was **appointed by Texas Governor Rick Perry** to **The Texas Judicial Council** and **The Texas Emerging Technology Fund**.

As president of the **Austin Junior Chamber of Commerce** (1983-1984), the U.S. Junior Chamber of Commerce recognized the chapter as the Most Outstanding chapter in the United States, and the **Junior Chamber of Commerce International recognized Richard as the Outstanding Chapter President in the world**.

He served on the board of directors of **Alpha Kappa Psi**, international professional business fraternity, and was a past chairman.

He has served on the board of many organizations including **The John Ben Shepperd Public Leadership Foundation, Boy Scouts of America, Muscular Dystrophy Association** and **Keep Austin Beautiful**.

Richard lives in Lakeway, Texas. His mission is to communicate timeless positive messages of proven principles helping people win every day.

RICHARD V. BATTLE RESOURCES

Navigating Life's Journey
Common Sense in Uncommon Times

If you liked **Conquering Life's Course**, you'll love this successor to it.

40 bite-sized, easy-to-read chapters of time proven principles will restore your **confidence** in your beliefs, **encourage** you to defend them, and **inspire** you to teach your **sacred values** to your loved ones. It will **lift your spirits** and **restore your hope** in America.

It includes 250 examples and 75 motivational quotes.

Available in paperback, Kindle, and audio editions.

Conquering Life's Course
Common Sense in Chaotic Times
Do you wonder if Common Sense is vanishing?

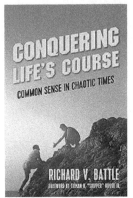

It will entertain and inspire the reader to think, laugh and undertake actions to realize a more fulfilling life.

If you or a loved one have given up on understanding the world of today, **Conquering Life's Course** is a must read. It offers reassurance to the reader that age old traditions and wisdom still rule over unproven theory.

It is concise, easy-to-read and offers invaluable insights that can be shared with the whole family.

Available in paperback, Kindle, and audio editions.

Unwelcome Opportunity –
Overcoming Life's Greatest Challenges

What do you do when you experience divorce, two heart procedures and a cancer diagnosis within ten months? It is the story of an ordinary man facing multiple life challenges in a ten-month period.

In it you will see an example of God's presence and provision that helped Richard Battle traverse this turbulent period of his life.

Available in paperback, Kindle, Nook and audio editions.

Surviving Grief by God's Grace

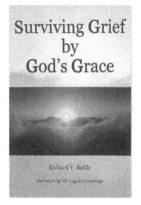

There is no greater loss in this world than the loss of one's child. This book is the first-person account of the author's loss of his first and then only child. It is a story of the grief, spiritual quest and grace that helped Richard and his family survive, and to live with hope for the future.

Available in paperback and Kindle editions.

The Four-Letter Word That Builds Character

Why are so many young people having a problem adapting to society today? Where have we gone wrong? Is it the parents or society in general? The Four-Letter Word That Builds Character can make a difference in this scattered and cluttered world. Based on the lessons learned from the author's first job and parental teaching of traditional values that have proven to be the foundation for lifelong success, this volume teaches 14 proven principles of a good work ethic and character.

Available in paperback Kindle and audio editions.

The Volunteer Handbook
How to Organize and Manage a Successful Organization

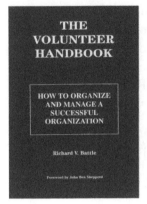

More than 75 topics that provide specific ideas that will help volunteer leaders maximize their efforts. Topics include: Long range, annual and event planning. Training board and prospective board members. How to recruit new members 10 steps to activate or reactivate a member 6 steps to building a successful team. How to motivate your membership. Effective Delegation. Managing non-performers.

Available in paperback

The Master's Sales Secrets
44 Strategies for Sensational Sales Success

Richard V. Battle offers business leaders a graduate-level class in what he's learned in over forty plus years in sales and sales management. Practical, sharp, and clearly communicated, The Master's Sales Secrets can be read cover to cover or referenced strategy by strategy.

Available in paperback and Kindle editions.

www.richardbattle.com